the
conscious
marketer

the
conscious
marketer

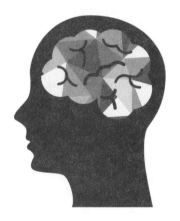

Inspiring a Deeper and
More Conscious Brand Experience

jim joseph

Author of the Award-Winning Blog and Book Series
The Experience Effect

www.amplifypublishing.com

The Conscious Marketer: Inspiring a Deeper
and More Conscious Brand Experience

For more information, please contact:
Mascot Books
620 Herndon Parkway #320
Herndon, VA 20170
info@mascotbooks.com

Library of Congress Control Number: 2019935280

CPSIA Code: PBANG0120A
ISBN-13: 978-1-68401-871-0

Printed in the United States

the award-winning books by jim joseph

JimJoseph.com

The Experience Effect
Engage Your Customers with a Consistent
and Memorable Brand Experience
May 2010

The Experience Effect for Small Business
Big Brand Results with Small Business Resources
January 2012

The Personal Experience Effect
Big Brand Theory Applied to Personal Life
August 2013

Out and About Dad
My Journey as a Father with All Its
Twists, Turns, and a Few Twirls
June 2015

Dedicated to my two children, Alicia and JP, who are now just starting their own careers. May you find as much fulfillment in your work as I have in mine.

Dedicated to my husband, Christopher, whose work allows me to continue learning and building my career, even after all these years!

Thank you for our life together.

Marketing is a spectator sport...

...and also a conscious contact sport!

contents

INTRODUCTION: *the experience effect*   *1*

MY WRITING STYLE: *if I had more time*   *7*

CHAPTER 1: *change is a constant*   *11*

CHAPTER 2: *a mix of art and science*   *17*

CHAPTER 3: *the latest force*   *23*

CHAPTER 4: *being conscious*   *27*

CHAPTER 5: *empathy*   *31*

CHAPTER 6: *conscious marketing*   *37*

CHAPTER 7: *politics aside*   *41*

CHAPTER 8: *a history of consciousness*   *47*

CHAPTER 9: *conscious, not conscience*   *55*

CHAPTER 10: *why now?*   *61*

CHAPTER 11: *the role of the ceo*   *69*

CHAPTER 12: *i don't want to go there*   *75*

CHAPTER 13: *dangerous territory*   *81*

CHAPTER 14: *running the organization*   *87*

CHAPTER 15: *crisis*   *91*

CHAPTER 16: *isn't this just targeting?*   *95*

CHAPTER 17: *becoming a brand*   *101*

CHAPTER 18: *the OGs of consciousness*   *107*

CHAPTER 19: *#tmwisc*   *111*

CHAPTER 20: *are you still advertising?*   *117*

CHAPTER 21: *two antiquated words*   *121*

CHAPTER 22: *two new words*   *127*

CHAPTER 23: *knowing your consumer*   *131*

CHAPTER 24: *conscious positioning*   *139*

CHAPTER 25: *social listening*   *143*

CHAPTER 26: *pioneers in emotion*   *149*

CHAPTER 27: *keep it real*   *155*

CHAPTER 28: *feeling tense*   *159*

CHAPTER 29: *finding your tension*   *163*

CHAPTER 30: *a note about touchpoints*   *169*

CHAPTER 31: *don't make them work*   *173*

CHAPTER 32: *conscious acculturation*   *177*

CHAPTER 33: *not just for big brands*   *183*

CHAPTER 34: *don't forget your employees*   *187*

CHAPTER 35: *personal consciousness*   *191*

CHAPTER 36: *be a benchmark brand*   *195*

about jim joseph: *marketer and dad*   *201*

the experience effect

NEVER MORE RELEVANT

Marketing is a spectator sport;
let's all learn from each other.
—Jim Joseph

WELCOME!

In my first marketing book, *The Experience Effect*, I explored a marketing approach that I have long believed and professionally embraced: a brand should be so much more than just a product and so much more than just functional product benefits.

A brand should deliver an experience, and that brand experience should be beyond compare.

By "experience" I don't mean a thrill ride or a pop-up store or a music festival sponsorship, although any of those could certainly be part of an experience. A true brand experience needs to be much bigger and more complete than any of those single events.

A full brand experience isn't a one-off encounter but rather a seamless flow of compelling interactions that moves from moment to moment as consumers continually, and repeatedly, buy in to the brand's premise and ultimately buy in to the brand's complete offering. At that point, the brand has become so much more than a collection of its physical attributes; it has magically become an experience that engaged consumers just can't live without.

This specific, curated experience turns a commoditized product into a differentiated brand for its targeted consumers—hopefully a very successful, differentiated brand with great consumer loyalty and longevity.

This is *The Experience Effect.*

I'm honored to have crafted and to teach a graduate course in integrated marketing at New York University, where we dissect the idea of the total brand experience and the difference between products and brands. We examine how brands become successful, and we try to learn from brands that seem to have failed along the way.

Marketing is a spectator sport, so we try to learn from brand successes and brand failures in the marketplace.

In addition to their homework every week, my students bring a recent example of what's happened in marketing for group discussion. We all learn a lot from each other, whether the brands are big or small. The range of brands we discuss is both global and endless.

I personally love examining brands and the impact of their marketing.

It's impossible for us not to look at Apple, Starbucks, and Amazon as shining examples of brands that consistently deliver a valuable brand experience beyond just the functional benefits of their products and services and beyond the functions of a tech device, a caffeine boost, or e-commerce delivery.

I personally and consistently go to Apple for the experience of feeling that I live on the tech curve with the latest gadgets to get the job done, no matter where in the world I may be traveling. I stop at Starbucks every morning because it helps me get mentally prepared for the day ahead, no matter where in the world I may be traveling. I shop at Amazon because I know I'll find what I want, when I want it, for a price that competes... with an overall shopping, checkout, and delivery experience that makes me feel contemporary. Now there's entertainment to buy, too, no matter where in the world I may be traveling.

Apple, Starbucks, and Amazon are obvious big brand examples that are easy to examine and they are generally the first brands we talk about in my class every semester. They are three go-to brands for many consumers and for my students too.

Now think deep into your own behavior and examine your own go-to brands.

Why do you continuously go back and choose those brands time and time again over others with similar functions? Think beyond just the product attributes and physical benefits.

How do your favorite brands make you *feel*?

Why are you loyal to your go-to brands?

What's the experience like when you engage with the brands you live with every day?

What's *The Experience Effect*?

Scotch & Soda (the fashion brand) is one of my go-to brands because it makes a man "of a certain age" like me feel a bit "with it." Scotch & Soda makes me feel like I've discovered a young indie brand with a fresh style that I can still pull off. The brand offers an age-appropriate fashion edge, which is important to me.

A brand should deliver an experience

Sure, I could get clothing from a variety of places, but I choose Scotch & Soda because it makes me *feel* like I stand apart, but without standing out and looking like I'm trying too hard. The experience of shopping at Scotch & Soda is consistently engaging as I see the associates wearing the clothes, each expressing his or her own individuality with the items. The associates bring merchandise that's not on the shelf out for me from the back room because they recognize me as a local regular (and they know I generally partake). The brand sends me alerts on items in stock as well as on sale items, and the brand's social media presence is continually in my feed, inspiring me to put my own style pieces together and to continually add to my own look.

And now the brand has just added a new subscription service for men to rent and try clothes before they decide to buy. Although "been there, done that," for women, it's a first for men.

Add it all up, and Scotch & Soda isn't just a shirt or a jacket or a pair of pants; it's a spirit that provides my own unique look. So I can look like me and not like everyone else.

Hence the Scotch & Soda *Experience Effect*. At least in my book. Literally, in my book!

Amazon and Scotch & Soda are big brand examples, but in my two sequels to *The Experience Effect*, I also wrote about how small businesses can build a brand experience and also how people can create their own personal brand using the principles of big brand marketing.

Hence *The Experience Effect for Small Business* and *The Personal Experience Effect*.

I continue the discussion almost every day in my blog, where I examine brand experiences as they hit the marketplace and we all discuss their effects.

Marketing is a spectator sport; let's all learn from each other.

In each book and each blog post, I ask readers, "What's your experience?" This is both a question and a challenge to answer for yourself and for the business/brand you lead. It's meant as inspiration to innovate and drive your brand forward.

While times have evolved and so much has changed since I wrote those books, the fundamentals of marketing remain in place. What seemed important to discuss in my first marketing book back then is actually even more important now.

Our lives have become increasingly and completely mobile, and we now have so many more channels to truly connect with our consumers. In fact, there is no more mobile; it's just life as we know it. We can now interact constantly in a two-way, three-way, group dialogue that never stops.

Most of us have our mobile devices next to us in bed! We check email, texts, and social media all day long—and all night long, in some cases. Most brands are monitoring and creating social activity around the clock, around the world.

Marketing has evolved to become a continual, always connected, multilayer experience where brands live with consumers and vice versa, within each other's expanding and dynamic networks.

The effect in *The Experience Effect* is even more powerful and more ubiquitous now. It's important that as marketers, we continually build upon it

Now it's time for me to take this all to an entirely new level of consciousness. Thank you for being here, and I hope you enjoy!

my writing style

If I had more time, I would have written a shorter letter.
—Blaise Pascal, French mathematician and philosopher

A BIT OF A CAVEAT as you start my book: I write in a conversational tone, as if I'm chatting with you. Because I wish I were chatting with you! I also write in respect of your time, because none of us have a lot of extra time on our hands. I'm not an academic; I'm a practitioner, so I speak and write as one.

You've been duly informed. Or warned, depending on your perspective!

When I first started blogging, I got a lot of positive comments about the brevity of my posts. I write to the point, or at least I always try to. I try to simply put a concept out there to spark thinking, not to overanalyze it, belabor the point, or say that I have it all right.

I refuse to drone on and on. One of my first editors at *Entrepreneur* told me to write longer articles. Ha! I always found myself saying, "*No!*" It's a lot harder to write shorter and more focused pieces than it is to write longer ones.

I like to focus.

So I purposefully wrote this book in easily consumable chapters, almost as if each chapter were a blog post. I want the book to flow and be easy to read so that you can read it on the train, plane, subway, or between meetings. One chapter at a time. On your own timetable.

This is my style, my brand.

One chapter at a time with one concept at a time. Some are shorter, and some are longer. Some more thought-provoking while some more lighthearted. All seamlessly building in a focused manner toward becoming a Conscious Marketer.

If I do wander off topic here and there, it's because I think I'm delving into something important. Bear with me and go with it!

I hope that ultimately I am able to spark some thinking for your brand.

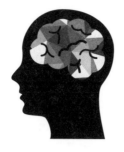

CHAPTER 1

change is a constant

I SIGNED UP FOR THIS

*Most people are scared to change the way they do business.
Find someone in your organization who isn't—they're
going to challenge your process like no one else can.*
—Mitch Lowe, cofounder of Netflix

THERE IS ONE WORD in life that I am completely comfortable with: change. Admittedly, most people aren't comfortable with change. I am. And in fact, when there isn't change, then I get nervous.

If there is one thing I've learned through the years, it's that change is a constant. As we go through the stages of our lives, we are in a constant state of change.

Think about it.

As children we start a new school year every fall with a whole new set of classes, teachers, friends, and schedules. Complete with new backpacks, pencil cases, and rulers. Well, now it's more like new mobile phones, online books, and note-taking apps.

I used to love the changes that came with going back to school every September. I still have a back-to-school feeling every Fall, looking forward to the change that always comes.

Then as young adults, we feel our lives change even more as we take on our first responsibilities at work and at home, all for the very first time.

Remember? For those of us who eventually have children of our own, we see how their lives change (as do ours) as we guide them through their choices.

Both of my children recently finished their studies and have started their new careers, one as a marriage and family therapist and the other as a marketer. I'm now an empty nester and bought a house on the other side of the country.

Life is a constant state of change. I love it.

What is true in our personal lives is certainly true professionally as well.

Most industries have undergone constant change, and that is certainly true of a career in marketing. I've been at it now for about thirty years, so I can attest to the tremendous amount of change in our craft year after year. The pace of that change has never been more rapid than it has been in the past few years.

Marketing is changing "at the speed of life," as we once said before we knew it would get even faster.

Marketing is in a constant state of change.

I tell my teams at the agency that if we aren't embracing change on a daily basis, then we aren't going to stay successful. No doubt about it, and I wouldn't have it any other way!

I'm inspired by brands that embrace and drive change as

well. I look at what Netflix has done with its brand over the years, and I'm in professional awe. Its team faced dramatic changes in home entertainment and not only went with the consumer and technology flow but actually reinvented an entire industry, with many other brands following.

I like to think about myself in a similar manner...embracing change and innovating along with it.

I'm fortunate to have experienced two major crossroads early in my career that have inspired me all along the way and have prepared me for the unprecedented rate of change that we are now facing in marketing.

One crossroad was decidedly purposeful, and the other was quite accidental.

I started my marketing career client-side in classic brand management at Johnson & Johnson Consumer Products. I say "classic" because I was trained formally and through mentors about the basic building blocks of marketing.

I learned about understanding consumer insights (I never really fully knew the word "insight" before). I became proficient in building a strategy (not an inherent skill, I can tell you that). And I discovered how data can lead to a great creative idea (well before we had the depth of data that we have today).

I managed brands in the Johnson's Baby Products portfolio, long before I had babies of my own. My skills deepened with extended stints in Oral Care (Reach toothbrush) and Skin Care (Purpose, Clean & Clear). I went on to do more brand management at Arm & Hammer in the toothpaste category there. I loved every single assignment, particularly launching new products. Over the course of that time, I launched nine new products in seven years.

Johnson & Johnson taught me to love marketing and to truly understand how to do it.

one brand and one brand experience

By starting out in brand management at a leading consumer packaged goods (CPG) company, I learned what it is like to build a brand in its totality.

I was responsible for the entire brand from start to finish, including the cost of goods sold, the advertising and promotion, the packaging, the formulas, and everything else in between. I was responsible for every aspect, not just one silo. I wasn't taught to see brand silos between advertising, promotion, packaging, or public relations. It was always just one brand. It was always just all marketing.

What was true back then is even more true today.

So today when I hear commentary about the future of integrated marketing, I have to laugh a little inside. From my perspective, marketing has always been integrated.

Integrated.

360.

Holistic.

Full circle.

Surround sound.

It's always been one brand and one brand experience to me.

I'm lucky I learned that from the start. I was purposeful in learning that from the start. I had mentors who taught me that from the start.

Thank you!

The other defining crossroad in my career was becoming "digital" so early.

Shortly after leaving client-side work, I started my own agency. We were designing brand strategy, creating full marketing campaigns, and even working on new product development for those very companies where I once worked. Because our clients trusted us so much, when these things called "websites" came along, they asked us to put them together for them. They didn't know how and neither did we, so we all had to quickly learn. There were no protocols or best practices, so we just dug in. We were humbly just a boutique agency in Princeton, New Jersey, making websites for the likes of the biggest brands on the planet.

We very quickly became what we now automatically call "digital."

After we sold the agency, we merged with a dedicated digital firm, which not only helped build my legitimate digital credentials even further but also gave us scale to take on even bigger digital projects. Now my even bigger team had the brainpower to deliver leading-edge thinking in this new and changing space called "digital marketing."

Change is a constant in a constant change of state.

Pretty soon, every campaign we conceived had a digital component. Social media wasn't in the picture yet, but as you can imagine, we had no problem embracing that when it came along. Even a guy like me at my age had no problem embracing it when it came along. I was already there in so many ways.

✳ I've embraced change every step of the way and have never resisted a new challenge at work. Even if I've had to create it myself!

Luckily, this series of events put me on a digital curve that I've never left. Not that we can really call it "digital" anymore. But we'll get into that later.

I've always greatly respected the brands that were able to drive the digital curve.

Like Netflix.

No brand knows the digital curve better than Netflix, and no brand has embraced change more. The brand rode the curve and drove the curve at the same time. Management continually changed its business model to mold to consumers' changing digital lifestyles and consumption of entertainment. As a result, Netflix put its analog competitors out of business and took over the market, reinventing itself and driving innovation in the process. Our at-home entertainment behavior and use of technology is a result of brands like Netflix, even though now there are too many to choose from.

I learned very early on in my career to embrace technology and to put it to use for my marketing ideas. So when advances continually come along, like VR, AR, and AI (virtual reality, augmented reality, and artificial intelligence, respectively), I don't really blink an eye. They're just better and more interesting ways to connect with consumers. They're just new ways to use technology to build a deeper brand experience.

I encourage you to do the same.

Just make sure you include a mix of art and science…

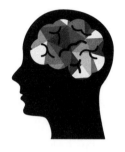

CHAPTER 2

a mix of art and science

KEEP LEARNING NEW TRICKS

In the modern world of business, it is useless to be a creative, original thinker unless you can also sell what you create.
—David Ogilvy, founder and CEO of Ogilvy Advertising

MY GUESS IS THAT if you're reading this book, then you're a big fan of marketing just like me. Or you're at least trying to become better at it, just like me. Marketing is an exciting, dynamic trade that has kept me hopping (and hoping!) for years. It's definitely kept me learning.

The inherent part about marketing that keeps this old dog learning new tricks is the beautiful mix of art and science that it embodies. Marketing's unique mix of form and function satisfies my every yearning to professionally explore, create, and grow. Every single day, year in and year out, after all these years.

Allow me to explain. The art part is easy to see, I suppose.

A massive amount of creativity is required to ideate and develop a marketing campaign that includes strategic positioning skills, creative writing abilities, and the knowledge to bring breakthrough ideas to life visibly. It's an art form equal to any other, albeit for commercial purposes.

Technology has allowed us to be even more creative and to constantly raise the creative bar through advances in interactive channels. Being successful in marketing means continually being more and more creative.

The science part may not be as readily noticeable, especially when you first start a career in marketing.

There is a clear and present methodology to creating campaigns that starts with research and data analytics. Here's where data (and what we used to call "big data") has changed the game in developing marketing campaigns.

We are now able to conduct research before, during, and after a campaign to not only influence the direction and calculate the results but to also course correct in real time as the campaign goes to market and consumers respond.

We can now react in real time and make the connection with our consumers even more meaningful, in the moment.

We also use data to better understand our consumer target much more deeply, demographically, attitudinally, and behaviorally. With data, we can get a much better picture of how our target lives their lives, breaking our consumers down into highly relatable segments, groups, and individuals.

Artificial intelligence (AI) is just starting to help us in data analytics. AI won't replace researchers or the teams who analyze

clear and present methodology

data, but it gives us ways to analyze even more. It gives us access to prefiltered and perhaps precategorized data sets that allows us the freedom to really dig into it all...perhaps giving us even deeper learning as a result.

AI is also starting to help us with the creative as well.

Again, AI won't replace creative teams, but it'll help them be even more creative in their work by deleting some of the more routine tasks that come from developing a creative campaign, leaving brain space for the real heavy creative thinking.

All the better to drive the creativity that will enhance consumer engagement that will drive sales. That's the end game, right?

A mix of art and science.

Then, of course, there's social media. That's an art and a science too.

Social media has changed *how* we interact with consumers,

and it's given them a voice that's just as powerful as brands themselves.

Traditional television advertising was long ago the dominant way to generate reach, but it was a one-way communication at best. These days, if you don't have a continual social presence, then dare I say you don't have a compelling brand at all. Now it's on a mobile device.

Just sayin'.

Social media marketing, not advertising, now makes a brand. Respect to David Ogilvy.

To succeed in social media and use technology to your advantage, you've got to be insightful, clever, quick, savvy, and creative.

A mix of art and science.

Frozen pizza brand DiGiorno is a great example.

Frozen pizza?

Who thinks about frozen pizza?

What does frozen pizza even taste like?!

Exactly. If I'm to be honest, the DiGiorno brand was lifeless, just sitting in the freezer case alongside other frozen pizza and frozen food options. No differentiation. No offense.

Suddenly, out of nowhere, DiGiorno comes alive through social media at a time when Twitter was just hitting stride and just becoming a part of pop culture. Someone on the social media team at DiGiorno knew exactly what he or she was doing!

Using technology and social media with a mix of art and science.

When NBC aired the first live broadcast musical (*The Sound of Music*) in 2013, DiGiorno was front and center on Twitter during the event, continually interacting.

"The hills are alive with the smell of DiGiorno pizza."

The brand sprang into real-time action, commenting right along with consumers as each musical number played out live on broadcast television. It was event or appointment television at its interactive and social media best, with DiGiorno enjoying the moment just like the viewers. Suddenly, the brand was fresh and relevant, just like its pizza!

"Rolf was the original delivery boy."

Gotta love it.

It wasn't advertising that brought the DiGiorno brand back to life; it was social media. It was real-time engagement directly with consumers, sharing a moment. Hopefully sharing a moment over a frozen pizza while watching live television.

DiGiorno sales soared for the first time in a very long time.

When you look at the flurry of activity on the social channels of KFC, McDonald's, Popeye's, and Wendy's, then you realize that this brand activity is required to stay relevant.

If social media changed how we interact with consumers, then mobile devices have completely changed *where* we interact with them...and it's put consumers in charge.

It's all on their terms now, as consumers go about their lives with multiple devices in their grasp day and night. If you're not a part of their mobile lives, then you definitely don't have a relevant brand. If you're not keeping up with the technology of mobile devices and how to creatively leverage it, then you definitely don't have a relevant brand.

This mix of art and science keeps us learning new tricks.

It won't be long before technology brings us another advance that will spark our creativity. It's only a matter of time before we will learn to bring a new mix of art and science to the brand's table.

It's a given.

But there's something else on the horizon that's making this all even more interesting...

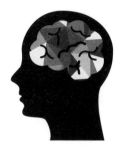

CHAPTER 3

the latest force

BRAND CONSCIOUSNESS

Our decision was not made for economic
gain, and our values are not for sale.
—Ed Bastian, CEO of Delta Airlines

FASTEN YOUR SEAT BELTS.

While there has been a daunting amount of change in marketing, it's certainly not over by any means. There is a new force that is driving even more change in how we market brands. While I can't exactly say that it came out of nowhere, it is fair to say that it's an entirely new phenomenon. And we're all just now getting used to it.

Blame it once again on social media and mobile devices, as both are partly responsible. But there's more to it than that.

It's not easy to describe or to sum up in a few words, but I'll give it a try. There's a new "brand consciousness" creeping into our marketing efforts that has never been here before.

Brand consciousness. Hmm.

As marketers we have a new level of awareness for what consumers think and feel about social, political, and economic factors and issues they face. Brands are paying attention to the collective world like never before, partially because consumers are paying attention too.

Brand consciousness.

It's a new aspect of marketing that is without a doubt driving how we will connect with consumers moving forward. It's the next era of change in the constantly changing field of brand marketing.

It's perhaps the deepest, most fundamental change that I've ever seen.

We are witnessing it on a weekly, if not daily, basis. Every new mass shooting brings it all back again. It's just one example.

Brands, many brands, are speaking up and voicing their opinions and, in some cases, altering their policies and changing their marketing based on consumer sentiment around this long-debated and highly sensitive issue of gun control. Not all consumers and not all brands are aligned on the same side of this emotional issue, which is why it's becoming so fundamental to some brands. It's fascinating to witness, in real time, how brands are taking a stand and how consumers are reacting to it.

Marketing is a spectator sport, and there are a few particular brands to watch about this issue.

Dick's Sporting Goods announced it will no longer sell assault rifles in its stores. Nor will it sell guns to anyone under twenty-one. Same with Walmart.

Delta Airlines flexed its economic power to influence

gun control policy in its home state of Georgia. The Georgia government wasn't pleased with Delta's use of its influence.

FedEx, who ships a lot of guns, attempted to stay neutral but by doing so was perceived to be supporting the NRA. FedEx, also based in Georgia, got caught in the middle of the issue regardless of its stance.

Dick's Sporting Goods, Walmart, Delta Airlines, and FedEx— brands at the crux of a societal issue like gun control.

We'd never seen anything like it.

Years ago, Starbucks announced that it wouldn't allow guns in its stores. While that move sparked responses from all sides, this new activity feels very different. Social media is on fire with consumers supporting or denouncing these actions. Social media is asking other brands where they stand on the issue too.

Consumers are asking for responses and making choices based on how brands respond to a lightning rod topic like gun control.

It's not just gun control, and it's not just about any one debated topic du jour. This isn't a brief moment that will suddenly disappear. Not at all. There's a much broader, more sustained change that is happening.

Change is a constant in a constant state of change.

I'm calling it *Conscious Marketing,* and I certainly am not alone.

Brand Consciousness. Conscious Marketing.

Let's explore this new concept of Conscious Marketing in its totality, dissecting how it's affecting brands and how it will affect your approach as a marketer.

Let's discuss what to do about it.

Let's examine how to add it to any brand, whether the brand

consciously wants to add it or not. I feel like there is no longer a choice.

For a brand to be successful in this yet again constant state of rapid change, then consciousness must be included in the total brand experience.

We must become Conscious Marketers. Starting now.

First, you have to put yourself aside...

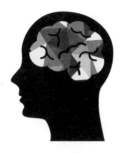

CHAPTER 4

being conscious

PUTTING EVERYONE ELSE FIRST

The best way to find yourself is to lose
yourself in the service of others.
—Mahatma Gandhi

CONSCIOUS.

If you look up "conscious" in Wikipedia, you instantly get a pretty clear definition of what "consciousness" means: "the state or quality of awareness, or, of being aware of an external object or something within oneself."

(Yes, I consider Wikipedia to be a resourceful resource, and I resource it all the time.)

Urban Dictionary has a similar explanation for "conscious":

"being in a state of awareness, alert, meaningful, with intent." Urban Dictionary also states that the antonym for "conscious" is "ignorant."

(Yes, Urban Dictionary is also a resourceful resource that I resource all the time.)

Being conscious means paying attention to the behaviors, attitudes, and feelings of others and taking them into consideration for your own behaviors, attitudes, and feelings.

Being conscious means being aware of how others may view you and your actions and taking their views into account. Being conscious means putting others' views before your own and putting yourself aside.

Yes, the opposite of "conscious" could certainly be said to be "ignorant." And I just love the notion of "intent" in all that we do (thank you, Urban Dictionary).

Being conscious is a human trait and a good one at that. Being conscious is something that we should all strive for in our lives and in our relationships. I'm not sure that as a society we are always successful at it, but I do believe that we, as individuals in our society, should all try. All the time. Especially right now.

I've tried to teach my two kids to be conscious. While I don't think they're terribly conscious of each other (ha!), I do think they've grown up to be relatively conscious people—particularly for their ages and for the experiences that they've had so far in life. For this, I'm a proud dad.

As a leader of a global communications agency, I also believe that it's my core job to be conscious. Being conscious is a requirement. Fortunately, I've learned how to be conscious from some of the best in the business. I've also learned from some who don't behave consciously at all. We can all learn from each other's strengths and weaknesses.

It's my job to be conscious of what's important to my teams and how that varies culturally around the world. It's also my job to be conscious of my clients' needs.

For me, being professionally conscious means putting the team's needs first, before mine. My team's needs are far more important to the success of the business than anything or anyone else's needs. I need my team to be successful, so I put its needs first. I try to make every decision consciously with my team in mind.

Mind you, it's not easy. Being conscious can be exhausting!

I've heard this perspective called "service leadership" or "leaders who serve." I think of it more as "conscious leadership."

Although he was not a marketer, I think of Gandhi when I think of service leadership. And while I don't think of him as a marketer, I do think of him as a brand. He had a positioning, an emotional benefit, and very compelling messaging. He promoted service leadership. Gandhi was a conscious leader. We can learn about service and consciousness from him.

I strive to be a conscious leader. I am in service to my teams. I'm very conscious of that.

Just like people, brands need to pay attention to the behaviors, attitudes, and feelings of their consumers, and they need to take them into consideration as they form their marketing plans. Brands need to be aware of how others view them and how others view their actions...taking all of that into account.

Brands need to be conscious.

Brands need to put their consumers' views before their own. Brands need to have intent in their marketing. There's that word "intent" again (thank you, Urban Dictionary).

I'm purposefully using the term "consumers" here for a very specific reason.

Consumers consume products, and they consume brands.

I could easily say "customers" or "clients" as well, but that feels more cold to me, while, admittedly, the definition is essentially the same. But when you think about your customers or your clients as consumers, it forces you to think about how to serve them, from both a product and a brand perspective. It forces you to think about how to frame your content and your messaging in a way that they will want to consume it.

Thinking about your customers or clients as consumers forces you to be in service to them. Conscious service. Conscious Marketing.

Being conscious is a new requirement that we've never really quite seen before, especially in such a universal way on so many dimensions. Being conscious in brand marketing has become a (permanent) paradigm shift in our industry and in our marketing craft. It's the newest change in how brands must behave, and it's here to stay. It's also the newest way in which leaders serve their teams.

Marketing is now just as much about being conscious as it is about selling products! Probably more so, if you actually want to sell products.

With empathy at its core...

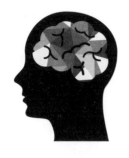

CHAPTER 5

empathy

THE SINGLE TRAIT

Leadership is about empathy. It is about having the
ability to relate to and connect with people for the
purpose of inspiring and empowering their lives.
—Oprah Winfrey (yes, that Oprah)

THERE'S NO DOUBT THAT we are living in challenging times.

They're certainly not the most challenging times ever, and we must remind ourselves of that every day. But there are days when it certainly feels like it.

There are days when all we see are the divides that separate us, and there are days when we long for "the good ole days." But I'm not sure they were so perfectly good back then, either. I remember I took a class from Gloria Steinem while I was in my MBA program at Columbia University, and she always said, "There's no such thing as 'the good ole days.'"

I get it, but these days aren't so good either way. And I'm an eternal optimist saying that. But we'll get through it. There you go, there's the eternal optimist again!

I will say that social media hasn't helped us feel much better about ourselves lately.

Yes, social media has given consumers a voice as powerful as any brand itself, if not more. Well, that same social media power applies to debating opinions and hashing out issues in public—constantly, all day and all night long. The debate never settles down and never goes away.

We feel it as people, we feel it as consumers, and we feel it as brands.

Which is why being conscious and Conscious Marketing has become such a requirement for brands. Consciousness helps us understand both sides of any given issue and how it affects our consumers. Consciousness helps us figure out that which divides us and perhaps how to bring us back together.

Why?

Consciousness gives us empathy.

In a nutshell, empathy is understanding what it's like to walk in someone else's shoes. That's not a Wikipedia definition as far as I'm aware, but it is a definition that I've picked up through the years that I know many others share. Empathy is about not only understanding what someone else is going through but having an appreciation for it as well.

Empathy is being a human and recognizing that others are human too.

So what would Wikipedia say?

"Empathy is the capacity to understand or feel what another

Empathy is being a human

person is experiencing from within their frame of reference, i.e., the capacity to place oneself in another's position."

Hmm. Empathy is basically consciousness. I could have titled this book *The Empathetic Marketer*!

Without empathy, we live in a bubble. Without empathy, we live in a silo where we only see our own point of view, where we judge everything against only what we know. Without empathy, we live alone. Without empathy, we have no consciousness.

Without empathy, we have no brand.

As people, perhaps we can live without empathy. It might be a lonely place, but we can exist. I would argue that a brand cannot live any longer without empathy. A brand without empathy simply won't exist.

As marketers, we have to be able to place ourselves in our consumers' position. We have to understand what they are going through in their lives and what forces are affecting how they live. Without empathy, we won't have understanding, and without understanding, we won't have enough knowledge to connect with our consumers.

Empathy helps break down our differences, and it will be what helps bridge our divided world.

I've heard it said that empathy is the single most important trait a marketer or any business leader can have to be successful. I would agree, and in fact, I could argue that it's the most important trait for any person.

I was recently asked what the single trait is that I look for when interviewing candidates. Single trait?

I said creativity.

Creativity opens the mind and helps to think about all the possibilities. Creativity solves problems and moves people forward. But truth be told, you can't really have creativity without empathy.

So in hindsight, I'd have to say that the single most important trait has got to be empathy.

I'm constantly interviewing new talent to join the organization, from junior to senior and from creative to account. And everything in between. I of course look for the core skills: intelligence, collaboration, analytics, work ethic, etc. Those are all table stakes to be successful in a role in marketing of any sort, including being creative. I initially screen for those skills to see who's even viable and who's really not. Sorry to sound so cold.

Once screened, empathy is the determining factor I use when choosing candidates. Empathy now determines if you'll get a slot. Empathy separates those who are qualified from those who will succeed. Empathy is what will make a candidate indispensable.

Everyone wants "empathy" on their team. Empathy means

you have the ability to truly relate to someone else, with a quest to help them out.

Brands need empathy to truly relate to their consumers. If you can't empathize with your consumers, how can you possibly know them?

How can you add value?

How can you expect them to embrace you?

You have to be able to walk in your consumers' shoes. Have I used the word "empathy" enough?

Empathy is the number one reason for Oprah's meteoric rise to success, from her early days on television to her dominant voice in popular culture to the public call for her run for president. Oprah is successful because she has empathy. Let her be our inspiration. Okay, she's also creative!

Empathy. The single most important trait in branding and in leadership today. Today more than ever.

So make it an active part of your branding...

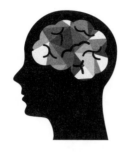

CHAPTER 6

conscious
marketing

ACTIVE AND INTENT

We're reinventing advertising.
—Marc Pritchard, CMO of Procter & Gamble

BEING CONSCIOUS. HAVING EMPATHY. Nothing really to argue with yet, right?

Right. It's what you do with it that really matters, however. That's where the debates all start. When you turn consciousness into being a Conscious Marketer, that's when the games all begin!

Being conscious is a mental state, but Conscious Marketing is a much more active state for brands. It's one thing to be conscious, but it's all together something else to do something impactful with that consciousness.

Conscious Marketing is active, not passive.

Conscious Marketing is more than just watching—it's doing. Conscious Marketing means making a true difference in consumers' lives, not just offering a function. Conscious Marketing means looking beyond the product.

Conscious Marketing is being active and having intent.

Let me show you what I mean, with Tide as a great example. Like any high-quality laundry detergent, Tide gets clothes clean, gets rid of stains, brightens whites, and makes clothes smell fresh. Any laundry detergent can do that.

As a consumer, there are many ways to learn about and understand the many functional benefits of Tide, the website being a primary source where every SKU is outlined and every feature is analyzed. There is no shortage of product information available on any of the Tide products!

When it comes to Conscious Marketing, there's so much more to Tide than just laundry products. Tide goes beyond its product benefits with its very own and very effective Conscious Marketing.

Through its many communications touchpoints, the brand Tide relates emotionally to consumers who take care of their families, no matter the type of family. The brand has consciously paid tribute to stay-at-home dads, for example, by authentically showcasing them and relating to their own unique situations. Just one example.

Tide does even more than just relate emotionally to the pressures of parenting. Tide is much more active than just that.

For example, Tide also acts as a first responder by sending truckloads of washing machines and dryers into areas where natural disasters have caused devastation. Tide helps those in need get their families' clothes clean. The brand calls it "Loads of Hope."

This is Conscious Marketing that is both active and full of intent.

In this manner, Tide continually proves that it's being conscious by fulfilling on emotional needs and by being an active member of communities in need. And, of course, Tide supplies great laundry detergent options.

So much more powerful than any thirty-second television commercial could ever be. Conscious Marketing, not advertising.

So yes, Conscious Marketing does mean becoming more active in the communities in which brands do business. Giving back is part of it, but Conscious Marketing takes it a step further to make sure brands are true members in their communities, right alongside consumers. Living and breathing the same air, so to speak. Not just doing business but doing what the other members of the community are doing as well. Not just writing a check, but actually physically and emotionally contributing to the community.

For Tide, it's showing up to help those in need get their families' clothes clean. For Tide, it's literally doing the laundry!

There's one key point buried in all of this that I have to make clear about Conscious Marketing, and it is absolutely certain—Conscious Marketing takes profit out of the equation. Profit is not a part of the discussion. That's not to say that brands shouldn't make money. It's not about making or not making money.

Publicly traded or private, brands are businesses, and they must generate a return to their constituents. Hands down. Even nonprofits make a profit; they are just required to funnel that profit back into the organization.

Conscious Marketing is not about not making money, but it is about not prioritizing it in a brand's actions.

Conscious Marketers prioritize their activities and prioritize their communications around their consumers' needs. While profit might still be there, it isn't front and center. Profit is not the central intent, even though brands still make money in the process.

Consciousness is the intent, and then so too will come profit.

Profit is not front and center; consumers are. The collective community is front and center. The brand's number one priority is satisfying consumers. Helping consumers. And yes, it's perfectly acceptable to make money in the process.

Tide has a profit motive for sure. As it's part of a publicly traded company (P&G), we can't expect otherwise. But Loads of Hope puts that profit motive on the back burner and instead prioritizes consumers who are in need, placing the brand in action to help. With Loads of Hope, Tide is right in the middle the community, all with active intent.

By the way, consumers don't want to think about brands any other way. They don't want to think about brands making money, even though they know that's the case. That's why Conscious Marketing has become such a shift in how brands go to market and how consumers bring brands into their lives. Because brands understand them and help them!

Tide has its own way of being a Conscious Marketer, but every brand gets to decide its own course...

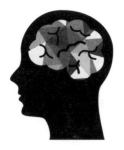

politics aside

NOT REQUIRED

*We don't support the immigration ban, and we have
been very public about it. Our simple view is that
Apple would not exist without immigration, so this is
a huge issue for us. So what do we do? We voice our
opinion and stand up—we don't sit in silence.*
—Tim Cook, CEO of Apple

BACK WHEN I STARTED my career at Johnson & Johnson, we
would never allow a brand to make a political statement. Never.
We were fearful of consumer backlash and a boycott. Because
those things happened all the time.

When I launched Clean & Clear, we were the first J&J
brand to ever advertise on MTV. Believe it or not, that network
was considered controversial at the time, and I had to fight
and fight hard to be able to advertise on it. "But how can I

market a product to teenagers if I'm not on their number one television network?" I pleaded over and over again to my senior management.

I eventually did advertise on MTV, and we did face some backlash from boycott groups. But we still didn't make a social or political statement; we were simply working to reach our audience where they were viewing their favorite programming.

No, we didn't have laptops or iPhones. And we didn't take stands on social issues.

Back then, we would never make a social/political statement because it just wasn't worth alienating what could be a huge portion of the audience. "Why would we do that?" we would ask ourselves. As a result, if there was any backlash, it was short lived.

Thankfully.

Obviously, times have changed. Change is a constant in a constant state of change.

We're seeing more and more brands take on political and social issues like never before. Many brands now have something to say about what's going on in our world, and consumers have something to say about brands having something to say.

I mean, seriously, we recently witnessed a brand join a lawsuit against a sitting president of the United States: Patagonia is suing the administration over the protection of our national parks. A lawsuit! From a brand to a political figure! I mean, wow! We've never seen that before.

And many other industries are choosing whether or not they want to support highly debated political issues like immigration. Because their employees are forcing them to think about it.

We also witnessed a brand that refused to release data on its users to the federal government. Apple held to its own privacy

we need to pay attention to it all

codes and wouldn't release information on Apple users for a government investigation. We've never seen that before, either.

Sexual harassment, freedom of speech, women's health, gun control, gay marriage, gender equality, gender identity, immigration, transgender rights, equal pay, tax reform...you name it. We're seeing brands enter discussions once thought to be off-limits. The list keeps getting longer and longer. And we're seeing consumers act accordingly, either picking or not picking those brands based on those positions. Or lack of a position.

For Patagonia, I would argue that it makes sense for the brand to take a political stand on protecting our national parks. Being outside and celebrating nature is part of what the brand is all about. So of course protecting those lands is an obvious choice for the brand and for those who consume it. I get it. I applaud it.

Restaurant chain Chick-fil-A is no stranger to taking a stand. The company and the brand was founded on the fundamentals of the company leadership's religious beliefs. The restaurants are even closed on Sundays, in observance, and the brand donates a portion of its profits to a religious-based foundation. The brand's beliefs are a core part of its business, and consumers either buy in to them or not. Certainly some consumers ignore the values-based business and just love consuming the food. Some are even conflicted about supporting a belief system that they don't personally believe in when consuming the food. Many are making conscious decisions either way.

While this new activity may be a trend, not everyone is buying into it.

Conscious marketing isn't for everyone. . .not everyone feels that brands should be entering these kinds of discussions. Some feel that the risk is too great, or some believe that it's just not a brand's place to be speaking up. I get that too. . .among other things, marketing is about making choices.

Kellogg's united its cereals and mascots to support GLAAD and its anti-bullying programs. Some applauded (like me!) and some said that LGBTQ+ issues shouldn't be on a breakfast cereal.

I, for one, embrace it. If you're going to be a conscious brand, then certainly it's fair game to have an opinion. You don't necessarily have to voice it in a public debate. You don't necessarily have to use it to shape all of your policies. But to me, it's all fair game, particularly if it's in line with your brand, such as with Patagonia or Chick-fil-A.

Consumers ultimately get to choose.

We'll talk more about this part of Conscious Marketing later, but I do want to put on record that taking a political stand is not necessarily a requirement like many would like to suggest. Nor is it off the table, as others would prefer. It's not as clear cut as all of that.

Let me repeat: Conscious Marketing does not require taking a political stand. Nor is politics the only form of Conscious Marketing, not by a long shot.

But something that is a requirement? Paying attention. We can't skip that anymore.

As marketers, we need to pay attention to it all, especially when our consumers are paying attention.

At the end of the day, Conscious Marketing is all about staying relevant in consumers' lives and staying relevant as a brand. For us in the field, it's about staying professionally relevant as professional marketers.

While being conscious and paying attention are relatively new concepts, they do have a deep history that we should examine.

It's always good to know our roots...

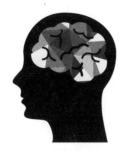

CHAPTER 8

a history of consciousness

HUMBLE BEGINNINGS

Giving feels good, but it's also good for the bottom line. Charity is a viable growth strategy for a lot of companies. Our customers get excited to be a part of what we're doing. If you ask anyone wearing TOMS how they first heard about us, most won't mention an advertisement; they'll say a friend told them our story.
—Blake Mycoskie, CEO of TOMS

ENTER JERRY LEWIS.

It's hard to say exactly when and where Conscious Marketing got its start. There were so many early pioneers on a number of fronts, each breaking barriers on different aspects of being conscious.

I may ruffle a few feathers here, but I'm going to say that Conscious Marketing started when brands started contributing to charities, and that was a long time ago. I'm going to stick my neck out even further and say that consciousness became a marketing "thing" when Jerry Lewis did his annual charity telethon for MDA (the Muscular Dystrophy Association).

The Jerry Lewis MDA Labor Day Telethon.

Jerry Lewis broadcast his telethon for the first time in 1966 (three years after I was born!). There were three national television networks at the time, and all three ran it every year over the entire Labor Day weekend. It was the only thing on television.

Can you imagine that happening today?

Watching the Jerry Lewis telethon was the entertainment event of the year, even more so than the Oscars or the Grammy Awards. All weekend long, celebrities would show up to perform, giving us a rare chance to see them live. They were there to support Jerry's very worthy cause. Brand after brand would also parade on stage to present Jerry with an oversized check, showing the amount of money either raised or contributed to his cause.

Jerry Lewis's telethon is my sense of when brands started being conscious. Not that we ever called it "consciousness" back then.

Brands supporting Jerry's cause were, in fact, being conscious. This telethon was probably one of the first times in modern marketing history where brands showed they cared about something other than their own brand.

These brands showed that they cared about helping Jerry Lewis find a cure. They also cared a lot about the exposure they were receiving from the record number of families watching the telethon every year! Conscious. Marketing. Conscious Marketing.

The telethon ultimately gave way to brands then supporting their own charities of choice, typically something near and dear to their own hearts, not necessarily someone else's.

Enter Marie Osmond.

I remember when I worked on Johnson's Baby Products in the late 1980s, we supported the Children's Miracle Network with a massive promotional program every year that included our retail partners. We also showed up with an oversized check for that telethon and presented it to celebrity host Marie Osmond, some twenty-five years after brands first did for Jerry Lewis and MDA.

Conscious Marketing at work, in my early work. I learned a lot from it.

Soon it almost became a requirement for brands to have charity components to their marketing, and that's when it all broke loose. Every brand picked a charity, and sometimes several charities, just to show how much it cared. I have had clients with dozens of charities on their rosters, just to have a roster of charities. Nothing wrong with that at the time. It was Conscious Marketing.

Looking back, though, I have to ask, "What was the impact of having so many charity initiatives?"

Was it really helping the cause?

Was it helping build the brands?

Was it effective marketing?

The problem is that this kind of laundry list (check off the boxes) charity work stopped being very conscious. It became charity for publicity's sake...logos on a page, a T-shirt, and a table for ten at a ballroom event for $10,000. The marketing lost its meaning. It lost its intent. It lost its consciousness.

The marketing lost its impact.

Yet, on a different dimension, there was another part of consciousness starting to bubble up. Brands started realizing that they should be more responsible to the earth—another form of being conscious. Brands started realizing that they needed to be more sustainable.

Enter Amway.

To my eye, the sustainability movement started with a company called Amway (short for "American Way") back in 1959, when the company launched an organic laundry detergent positioned as safe for the environment. It was called LOC (Legacy of Clear).

Amway started as a multilevel sales and marketing organization, where everyday consumers could sell the products to their own network of friends and family. Amway was not only an early form of being eco-friendly but also an early form of social networking—long before most were eco-friendly and long, long, long before we had social networks (of the online variety).

Voilà (well, maybe not "voilà")—sustainability was born. We suddenly became conscious of responsible manufacturing and of responsible distribution methods (among other sustainability factors) overnight.

Every brand on the planet started demonstrating how it was being good to the planet.

Activist organizations and consumer groups started asking questions and investigating brands' impact on the environment. "Carbon footprint" became both a buzzword and a measuring stick; reducing your carbon footprint became a conscious movement.

Perhaps I'm exaggerating here, but within a matter of what felt like a decade, sustainability went from being an emerging issue to a hot-button initiative to an absolute requirement. We went from being naive to being conscious to being purposeful through the efforts of some very dedicated people and organizations.

Sustainability became the norm. Being conscious of the environment became the norm. Those that participated prospered. We proved that Conscious Marketing can work, especially when it involves being good to the planet.

Amid the sustainability movement came another thing called CSR (corporate social responsibility), a—what I will—call catch-all for all that is conscious. CSR became an umbrella term for any responsible marketing: charity work, sustainability, community relations, and even employee satisfaction and retention.

CSR is indeed a form of Conscious Marketing and is the predecessor to it, but it's still not the complete picture.

Conscious Marketing has gotten much bigger than that. Conscious Marketing now has a much bigger effect on our consumers than anything that has preceded it.

Let's try to bring this all to life a bit.

Enter Tom.

Here's a little story in the evolving history of charity, sustainability, CSR, and Conscious Marketing. It's a tale of the Toms.

The first Tom is Tom's of Maine, as in the organic toothpaste brand. The brand and the company Tom's of Maine are both rooted in consciousness and both founded on sustainability. The brand was a client of mine at one point, so I know a bit of its history, and I know its work to be sincere and authentic. Tom's of Maine is one of the first brands to be holistically created to be sustainable, with a keen understanding (consciousness) of its impact on the environment. Annual sustainability reports to highlight the brand's responsible policies (and reduced carbon footprint) became the norm because of brands like Tom's of Maine, who was among the first.

The second Tom is TOMS shoes. The TOMS shoe brand literally invented the "buy one, give one" Conscious Marketing phenomenon. TOMS shoes turned the ever-so-popular "buy one, get one free" (BOGO) promotion on its heels (ha!) by giving a free pair of shoes to a person in need. Buy one, give one. Say what?! Yes indeed, when you buy a pair of TOMS shoes, you are also buying a pair for someone else who can't afford or access shoes. Breakthrough marketing concept. I bought several for myself and for my daughter. It felt good. It felt conscious. It had an effect on us!

The third Tom is Tom Tom Club, which has nothing to do with any of this except the band recorded one of my favorite songs from high school. I mean, how can you not like a song that says, "What you gonna do when you get outta jail, I'm gonna have some fun." 'Nuff said. Back to the point.

What works for big brands also rings true for entrepreneurs and small business owners.

One more Tom: Take Thom Boy Properties in Palm Springs, California. This brand is a dynamic duo that restores local Palm Springs midcentury period architecture, keeping it true to the community's heritage. Thom Boy Properties practices its own form of Conscious Marketing by staying true to the legacy of what it means to be in Palm Springs. It's Conscious Marketing because the brand gives those who want to move to Palm Springs a way to thrive in the unique aesthetic. Thom Boy is the hottest property development company in Palm Springs today because the brand is conscious about its work to keep the integrity of the town's heritage intact.

By the way, I bought a place in Palm Springs, California, and it's become my retreat of all retreats. That's *retreat*, not retweet!

So there you have a tale of the Toms, with their various forms of Conscious Marketing through the years.

Now keep in mind that much of this comes from a time when brands didn't tout their own Conscious Marketing. Brands didn't make a big deal or make public their conscious efforts to be responsible or sustainable or do charitable work. At the time, it was viewed as being pompous to promote the good your brand was doing.

"If you're doing good for others, then you shouldn't brag about it," was the prevailing thought at the time.

Back then, brands were humble about being conscious.

Humility is an art form and often stems from really great work, so there's no need to brag about it. Or so we thought.

These pioneer brands, and many others, were being humble about their great work at the time. Shouting about it would have diminished its importance and clouded its impact at the time. We can learn a lesson in humility from the work of these brands.

But now, in our times, being conscious is expected, and we need to talk about it.

Brands have learned that they have to pay attention to stay relevant. Consumers want to know what brands are doing to be conscious, and they want to hear about it directly from them. They want to see Conscious Marketing in action.

They want to see and feel how a brand's consciousness is affecting their lives.

But it's still good to be humble. Being humble is a consciously positive trait for people and for brands. We just don't have to be silent anymore. Humble no longer requires being silent.

Times have changed, and we've evolved to the point where doing good and being conscious are givens—and it's very much public.

Doing good and being conscious. Essentially, we've evolved from having a conscience to being conscious.

Spell check...

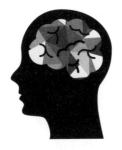

CHAPTER 9

conscious, not conscience

IT'S NOT RIGHT VERSUS WRONG

*Awareness of the dangers of texting and driving has increased,
but people are still doing it. With this expanded effort, we
hope to change behavior. Together, we can help save lives.*
—Randall Stephenson, chairman and CEO of AT&T

CONSCIENCE VERSUS CONSCIOUS.

My, what a difference a few letters make: *-ience* versus *-ious*.
Conscience versus conscious.

Wikipedia! A core definition of conscience: "Conscience
is an aptitude, faculty, intuition, or judgment that assists in
distinguishing right from wrong. Moral judgment may derive
from values or norms (principles and rules). In psychological
terms, conscience is often described as leading to feelings of

remorse when a human commits actions that go against his or her moral values and to feelings of rectitude or integrity when actions conform to such norms."

Having a conscience is not the same as being conscious.

Having a conscience means worrying that what you are doing is the right thing to do.

Like the early forms of sustainability—those brands had a conscience. Those brands wanted to do what was right for the planet. They were worried about their impact on the environment. They had a conscience.

Being conscious is different than having a conscience.

Being conscious is being aware of the bigger picture of what's happening in the world and being aware of your part in it. Whether that world is the planet, a community, a group of people, or someone's singular life. Whatever your "world" is.

Consciousness isn't about right or wrong, like conscience is.

A brand can be extremely conscious but not have a conscience or not care if what it's doing is wrong. A brand can also have a conscience but not be conscious of the world around it at all.

Some very conscious brands have done some pretty bad things, particularly to the environment. Or at least they haven't appeared to have handled issues with a conscience, seeming to not care about what's wrong in their actions.

I suppose the same could be said of people too!

We've all seen it, so I don't need to call it out by name. Legal cases abound.

Like when a transportation brand seemingly altered its regulatory submissions for financial gain. Or like when a consumer goods brand seemingly delayed a product recall to avoid excessive costs, even though it knew consumers were

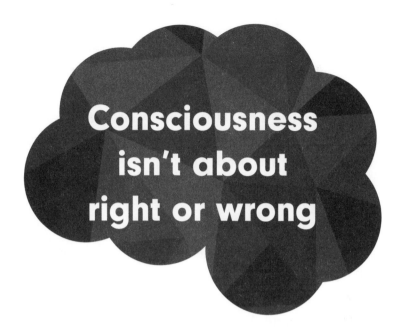

Consciousness isn't about right or wrong

potentially getting hurt. Or like when a food brand seemingly delayed negative safety data until it knew it was affecting a big enough population to hit a government threshold for required action.

Required action as opposed to action with a conscience.

Conscience versus conscious.

So it's important not to confuse having a conscience with being conscious. I'd argue that a brand needs to have both. It needs to be conscious and have a conscience.

I suppose the same could be said of people too!

Like when you go to a restaurant and the service is slow, so they comp you dessert to make it up to you. Conscious and conscience. Makes you want to go back, even though the experience wasn't perfect, right? Right.

Or like when AT&T ran a public service announcement (PSA) campaign to educate people on the dangers of texting and driving. The brand offers texting as a core service and was conscious of the fact that its consumers were using the service in a dangerous way. So the brand had enough of a conscience to know that it had the ability to help save lives. AT&T showed us that a brand can be conscious and have a conscience at the same time. It was a pioneering move.

Makes you feel better about AT&T as a responsible brand, right? Your call.

We often see this play out when there's a brand crisis. In these tough times, we see whether a brand has a conscience and if it's conscious.

Is the brand aware of the effect of the crisis (is it conscious)?

Does the brand feel responsible for it (does it have a conscience)?

Even more importantly, does the brand feel responsible for fixing it (is it conscious and does it have a conscience)?

Example: Facebook (as in the social network)

Facebook has seen its fair share of crises when it comes to data privacy. Many have accused the brand of not having a conscience with its sale of data to third parties. That certainly might be the case; I'll leave that to the court of social opinion. But I will certainly argue that Facebook wasn't conscious of how people truly feel about their privacy. As the biggest social network in the world, that lack of consciousness was a big miss, whether the brand had a conscience or not.

Facebook's use of its user data has called its conscience into question, bringing a new level of consciousness to privacy—perhaps a long time in the making.

That's not to mention how users (and non-users) perceive the use of Facebook for political advertising and its effect on elections. There's another one!

Makes you feel different about Facebook, right? Your call.

Example: Odwalla (as in the juice brand)

Odwalla is a great example of a conscious brand with a conscience. Back in 1996, the brand's apple juice was tied to a breakout of E. coli that killed a child and sent dozens to the hospital in the United States. Taking a page out of the infamous Tylenol crisis from more than a decade prior, the brand immediately recalled all products containing apple or carrot juice, consciously accepting full responsibility.

Odwalla, with a conscience, took its responsibility even further. The CEO promised to pay all medical bills for those affected. The brand held daily press briefings to track the crisis and released a full marketing campaign to explain the situation. A very conscious response with a conscience.

Makes you feel different about Odwalla as a brand, right? Your call.

It's always up to the opinion of the target audience...

why now?

NOT JUST MILLENNIALS

Uber is the official ride of pop culture.
—Bozoma Saint John, chief brand officer of Uber

IF YOU'RE LIKE ME, then you're probably wondering how we got to this place. Where did this new consciousness come from?

We're now living in a world of total transparency where a rapidly changing news cycle keeps us on our toes.

I don't watch network news at the end of the day anymore; I have Google News that curates my news. I tap in to Google News all day long, not just at night to see what happened that day. I'm looking at my news feed all day long because the news is changing all day long. I look at it first thing in the morning, right after Instagram (!), to see what happened overnight. Not to mention when there's an election cycle!

Because yes, news happens all day and all night long, not just from 9:00 a.m. to 5:00 p.m. EST. Sounds obvious, but this wasn't always the case. Back in the day, we got our news at 6:00 p.m. EST. Now it's no longer "news" by the time 6:00 p.m. EST rolls around.

We now live in a global news cycle where we all connect with each other. I have friends and colleagues living in different countries, so when something happens in their world, I want to know. Plus, I know it's going to affect my world too. We are all connected. I run a global business, so I very consciously keep a world view on what's going on in the news and how it impacts my teams, my colleagues, and my clients. That's my business.

By the way, brands are no different…brands are living in this exact same world.

Brands are interacting in a zone of total transparency where a rapidly changing news cycle keeps them on their toes. If they're smart, they're also tracking the news 24/7. We follow the news for all our clients around the clock.

Not too long ago, brands would more simply monitor the news for mentions of the brand. Now brands must do more than passively monitor. They must actively listen to all commentary that may affect their business and the lives of their consumers. Brands have to be conscious that the lives of their consumers is their business.

But why now?

What's changed?

We can't just blame it all on the digital revolution because that would be only partially right. That's too simple of an explanation.

The digital revolution has allowed us to track and see world events in a flash, that's for sure. It's also changed how we research, select, and purchase products and services—not just in goods distributed via Amazon but also in hospitality, automotive, education, and even health care. Even some of that we can now get via Amazon and Costco, for that matter.

The digital revolution gave rise to social media, and that did indeed change our lives. Not just the social channels like Facebook, an early catalyst. But also all of the innovative advancements that happened because of the initial social media and how we all embraced it.

Likes...shares...bloggers...reviews.

Social media gave consumers a voice.

They've always had a vote in terms of buying or not buying a product or service. But social media gave them not only a vote but also a voice. That voice became more powerful than anything, because that voice influences other voices and votes. That voice is influential and can impact opinion at any step along the process of selecting a product or service.

That voice can determine the future success of a brand, not just the sales that are happening today.

So when a brand releases a new piece of marketing that really inspires us, consumers use their voice to cheer it along and pass it to others. And when a brand does something that's even the least bit sensitive, consumers are quick to track it down and comment on it.

In a social media minute.

So can we blame it all on social media?

Not entirely. Most people call out millennials. What about them? Is that who's done all of this?

I won't drone on and on and blame this all on the millennial generation either, because that too would be far too simple. There have been more than enough blog posts, articles, white papers, and books written about the effect of the millennial generation. I've written a few myself. I think it's fair to say that we're collectively tired of placing everything on the millennials...so much so that now we're starting to focus on the next generation behind them. Gotta love us marketers!

But the truth is that the millennial mind-set has brought Conscious Marketing into our psyche. I purposefully say "millennial mind-set" because it's not just about chronological age or the exact range of years within which you were born.

Millennial mind-set.

In fact, we can't just market to millennials, even though that's all I hear these days from clients. We are challenged to market to consumers of all generations, including the baby boomers, who are still vital, as well as the up-and-coming generation after the millennials, who are just now exerting their influence. They are an interesting bunch too. In the US, they will be the first generation where there will be no single majority.

Rather than target an age group or a demographic, I prefer to go for an attitude, a way of being, or a point of view—that's ageless.

For me, and for many others, that's the millennial mind-set, regardless of the person's age.

The millennial mind-set, in my book (and this is my book), is about igniting change. It's about not accepting the status quo, and it's about not reaching compromise. It's about using the digital revolution, leveraging social media, and operating with an open mind to move past what's typically been possible.

It's about having it your way, without compromise. And being willing to pay for it, without hassle. Along with the many others you choose to incude in your network.

Millennial mind-set.

Why should I stand out in the pouring rain trying to hail down a cab when I can just sit in my apartment and call a car on demand? A nice car. A car that I don't have to fumble through my bag to find my credit card to pay for. A car that I know is just minutes away because I can track its ETA on my phone. A car in which I don't have to give directions to the driver. A car that I can call when I leave my mobile phone in the back seat and then get it back. Been there, many times over.

A car my way, without compromise. Easy to pay for, without hassle.

Millennial mind-set.

Why should I spend time hunting down friends who owe me money? There's an app for that!. The digital and social revolution. Money management my way, without compromise. Easy to pay for (or not pay for), without hassle.

Millennial mind-set.

This is the millennial mind-set of change: leveraging digital innovation to improve our lives and then using social channels to spread the word.

Having it your way, without compromise. Easy to pay for, without hassle. Millennial mind-set.

The millennial mind-set also brought us the transparency we live in now.

The millennial mind-set wants to see every aspect of each other's lives, including who paid for what at dinner last night so that you can pay him or her back on mobile. And who's friends with whom to see if you want to be friends too. And who likes this brand or not, so you can decide too.

That transparency pertains to brands as well. The millennial mind-set wants to know what brands are all about: where the brand contributes, whom the brand friends, and what the brand likes. The millennial mind-set makes brand decisions based on brand behaviors, not just product benefits.

Millennial mind-set. Not age, but mind-set.

Take a look at the brand Lululemon.

Lululemon basically started the concept of bringing fashion to athletics and bringing athletics to fashion. In this case, yoga clothing that soon became activewear. Then it evolved into gym wear and street wear.

Athleisure!

Lululemon built its entire brand to help women feel good while exercising and to feel good wearing athletic clothing inside and outside of the gym (or the yoga studio).

Having it her way, without compromise. Millennial mind-set. Mind-set, not age.

Lululemon has become a lifestyle brand, with women (and now men too) buying in to the entire product line—the yoga pants, for sure, but also the mats, hats, bags, jackets, and water bottles even if they don't actually do yoga!

The product benefits are all there, including ABC (antiball crushing) pants and shorts for men. See, even products have an emotional benefit!

Lululemon fans are true fans and loyalists.

Lululemon has built a cultlike community that has stood by the brand even when there's been controversy. And there's been drama—like the quick turnover of its CEO or new fabrics that become see-through when women stretch. And there's a lot of stretching in yoga!

But every year on International Women's Day, Lululemon is present, offering inspiration for every woman to be the best she can be, consistent with its founding principles.

Lululemon caters to the millennial mind-set and is a Conscious Marketer.

The millennial mind-set wants to see a brand's values to

make sure it aligns with their own. I'm no millennial by any means, but I do have a millennial mind-set. I value brands more when I see that my friends value them. I value brands more when I see them support something that is important to me. I value brands more when I see them in action.

I value brands when I know what the CEO stands for too…

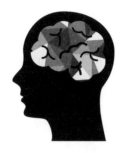

CHAPTER 11

the role of the ceo

THE VOICE OF THE BRAND

*For better or worse, our company is a reflection
of my thinking, my character, my values.*
**—Rupert Murdoch, founder, chairman, and CEO of News
Corporation**

THE BUCK STOPS with the CEO.

It always has, and it likely always will. The CEO is the chief of the chiefs and is ultimately responsible for all aspects of the business, including the brand. The CEO is ultimately responsible for sales and profits. The buck stops with the CEO.

A CEO's job never ends, and it's all encompassing.

Some of the historically famous CEOs—Steve Jobs, Bill Gates, Jack Welch, Richard Branson, Rupert Murdoch—all became synonymous with the company they ran or, in some cases, continue to run. It's impossible to separate the person from the company when there's a high-profile CEO involved.

There are more and more high-profile CEOs now than ever, and they're no longer just men, or classically trained, or tenured in their field of choice. Thankfully!

The CEO is ultimately in charge of every single aspect of the organization. Sure, there's a suite of talent surrounding the CEO, but ultimately the CEO makes the call. While the CMO takes care of marketing, the CTO takes care of technology, and the CSO takes care of business strategy, it's ultimately the CEO who lives or dies by it all.

The CEO makes the final call.

But the CEO has a new job, making the role even more important and even more difficult.

The CEO is also the face of the company. While being the "face" of the company may not be completely new, there is a new dimension to it that's critical to the success of the brand.

Now with Conscious Marketing, the CEO has even more responsibility. The CEO has to be conscious, too, and has to speak on behalf of the company's consciousness.

The CEO is now the "voice" of the brand in addition to being the "face of the company." The CEO no longer just represents the company, but he or she also represents the brand as well. The CEO is the face and the voice of the company and of the brand.

Face and voice, company and brand. CEO. The buck stops with the CEO.

Some might say that this was always the case. True.

But the CEO has generally been just an internal voice for the employees, stockholders, and suppliers and externally for shareholders and analysts. The CEO has always commented on the state of the business and the future outlook of it, but only to those closely associated with the business. Sometimes the CEO speaks to key customers in a B2B (business-to-business) industry or consumers in an open forum, but not on a mass-market scale. Not until now, anyway.

I've always looked up to my CEOs, yearning for inspiration and vision for where the company is going. But I never saw my CEOs communicating much outside of the company.

The millennial mind-set we spoke about has given the CEO a new role: brand communications officer. Internally and externally. Privately and publicly. With consciousness now a requirement, we could also say that the CEO is the chief consciousness officer too. Comes with the territory, whether he or she is equipped for it or not.

Chief consciousness officer! The CEO has always had a big job, but now it's even bigger!

The brand can live or die based on the voice of the CEO, what is communicated, and how it is communicated. The brand and company's values are the CEO's values, and vice versa. That's the perception, whether it's reality or not.

Take a look at the company and brand Papa Johns. Their CEO infamously and perhaps purposefully tied his own values to the brand and both have diminshed.

I would argue that the CEO's values should reflect those of the consumer, too, or there's trouble on board. Now that's new territory for sure. Yup, that's being a Conscious Marketer. Whether the CEO is equipped for it or not.

The millennial mind-set wants to know what the CEO is all about. The millennial mind-set wants to know that the beliefs of the CEO trickle down into the organization and become a part of the products and services that it offers. The millennial mind-set wants to know that the CEO's values also represent those of its employees.

Millennial mind-set. Mind-set, not age.

When all are aligned: branding. Powerful branding. Conscious Marketing.

Martha Stewart is a pioneer in this space.

She was the founder of Martha Stewart Living Omnimedia and at one point was also the CEO. Martha was not only the leader of the organization but the voice of the brand as well. She was the brand, through and through. Despite her ups and downs, she still remains the voice of the brand and still guides the brand.

Airbnb is another great example.

Airbnb has a very vocal CEO, who talks about wanting to deliver equality in hospitality anywhere in the world. Like Uber, Airbnb changed the course of the hospitality industry and channeled the millennial mind-set to alter how consumers go about booking and experiencing vacations.

The CEO's values are tied to the brand's values, which draws in consumers.

Chief values officer?

When natural disasters hit, Airbnb is right there, with the CEO announcing immediate relief efforts. When there's news of inequality somewhere in the world as it relates to hospitality, the CEO speaks up with support and reinforces the brand's values.

The CEO does more than just communicate brand values. He also motivates others to participate as well. Individual Airbnb properties can get involved with an initiative called "Open Homes," where they literally "open [their] heart and [their] home to evacuees." Individual Airbnb properties donate their homes for those who need to escape the damage of natural disasters or the danger of political issues.

These Airbnb properties are living the CEO's and the brand's values. Millennial mind-set, not age.

The property owners can also pick causes they want to support, aligning their own personal values with the brand to help the community. This is Airbnb joining forces with its audiences, consciously addressing what's going on in the world, with its CEO as the master voice of the brand.

Airbnb is a Conscious Marketer.

So all the king's horses and all the king's men can put together a brand, but it's up to the CEO to make sure it has the effect that the organization wants. It's up to the CEO to consciously communicate it appropriately. With full transparency. With a strong face and big voice for the company and brand.

Chief consciousness officer!

Not all CEOs are equipped, and that's part of the dilemma…

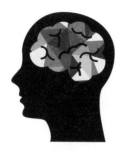

CHAPTER 12

i don't want to go there

THE RISK OF STAYING SILENT

We're going to continue to embrace our belief in diversity and inclusion, just how important that is to our company. But we're also going to make sure our focus on safety is unwavering.
—Brian Cornell, CEO of Target

WE'VE SEEN IT HAPPEN so many times now. Brands get demolished on social media for making the wrong move or saying the wrong thing. We see it almost every week.

As a result, many brands are afraid to tread into these Conscious Marketing waters because they've seen too many brands die in the court of social media opinion. Brands are right to be cautious. I know there are a lot of people out there saying,

"I don't want to go there." I know because I see it constantly in the comments on my blog. I don't blame anyone for not wanting to go there.

But I don't think you have a choice anymore, so you have to make sure your brand is well equipped.

There are many marketers who think it's safer to stay silent, remain neutral, and keep out of the fray. They don't want to turn anyone off from their brand, so they try to make sure that they don't do anything that would upset anyone. I don't blame them.

It's almost impossible to never upset anyone, but it's not as scary as it may seem.

Please remember that Conscious Marketing isn't necessarily about taking a stand on a sensitive issue or aligning along a political point of view. It's about having an awareness and understanding of what's going on in the world and then actively deciding how to participate as a member of the community. As we discussed, that might indeed include taking a stand or expressing your values and views. But it doesn't have to. I wouldn't blame a brand if it didn't take a stand, provided it is at least aware.

Sometimes a brand shouldn't take a stand on an issue. Sometimes a brand should simply be more conscious and think about the issue more before it ever jumps in—if ever. Sometimes a brand should know when to keep quiet.

Many marketers don't want to "pull a Target."

Remember when the Target brand took a stand against transgender access to bathrooms in North Carolina? Considerable backlash took place, and many people attributed the company's following sales decline to its stand on the issue. But in the end, Target stayed true to its opinion and even invested $20 million in bathroom upgrades across many of its stores. Target took the

make sure your brand is well equipped

kind of stance that many brands avoid—the kind of stance that many brands will try to avoid at all costs. Nike has consistently taken this kind of risk, more recently in its use of spokesperson Colin Kaepernick. The brand didn't back down when faced with the pressure to retreat, and flourished as a result. But not every brand wants to do that.

You may likely be one of those marketers.

I hear you. I was there myself at one point. But I have to be honest and say that we don't really have a choice anymore but to be more conscious.

Now that's not to say that you have to take an activist stance on a hot political issue, like transgender rights. Remember: I said that this doesn't have to be about politics at all.

But you do have to be conscious, because even if you don't intend to insert yourself into a sensitive topic, you may find yourself right there in the middle of it by accident. Or a consumer or consumer group may pull you in. Or a competitor may create guilt by association for your brand.

Or, in the case of the Target issue, a transgender individual may step into your establishment and ask to use a particular bathroom.

What are you going to say?

What if there are people watching who then post your response on social media for all to judge?

What if you are suddenly in the middle of an issue you didn't want to tackle?

By the way, the millennial mind-set is going to ask you for your opinion anyway, so you have to be prepared on some level. So even if you don't want to jump in, you still may have to answer questions like:

- What are your brand values?
- What does your brand stand for?
- What's your CSR program?
- Do you know what's important to your consumers?
- Do you support this particular issue or that particular issue because it affects your consumers?

There it is.

This is why you can't avoid it all completely. You don't have to go public with it and stand on a pedestal, but you do have to be prepared.

You absolutely have to know how your consumers feel. You absolutely have to be conscious. You absolutely have to be accurate, honest, and transparent.

If there's something that's important to your consumers, then you have to know about it. While you may not want to address it, you have to know it's out there, if only to avoid a fatal mistake when eventually coming up against it.

Remember that being conscious is also being active. Even if you don't want to take a stand, you need to be prepared with an action plan in case you get pulled in. Preparedness is a part of being conscious, whether you're a vocal participant or not.

Confidentially, we had a client that got unknowingly pulled into an industry crisis where some major health issues were erupting. Although my client's brand had nothing to do with the issue, it was still a crisis in the making, and it was spreading fast. Our client's brand, while completely uninvolved and unaffected at first, suffered pretty quickly from guilt by association.

Sales dropped precipitously as a result of activities from the other brands in the category. Luckily, we were monitoring the situation, and although it came out of nowhere, we had enough advanced notice to prepare. While we weren't willing to make a public statement for a variety of reasons, we were ready with a full response plan to manage the issue wisely and eventually get sales to rebound. Our client wanted to stay out of the fray, but it wanted to stay protected. It wanted to protect its consumers, too, with accurate information. Our consciousness and preparedness kept us out of the story and allowed us to keep an arm's length from a weighty issue while also keeping our consumers safe and informed. Sales did in fact rebound.

Consciousness in motion, without having to take a stand or get too involved.

We were being Conscious Marketers.

Although we didn't take a stand, we were still actively conscious in the moments leading up to and after the issue, knowing that we were affected merely because we did business in the category.

This is even more important in our era of "disinformation" or what some call "fake news." All brands can fall victim to it, and all brands can be capable of inaccuracy. Transparency is key to both avoid and combat disinformation. Let consciousness rule!

Being conscious is now a requirement, as is Conscious Marketing. And if you want your marketing to have a positive impact on your business, then you have to actively work toward being a Conscious Marketer.

If you don't, the effect could be catastrophic.

The millennial mind-set (regardless of age) says we must be informed and act appropriately. If we aren't, then we run the risk of looking uninvolved, uninformed, and unaware.

Or even worse, the brand loses its relevance.

So put aside your fears and jump into the life we now live. Be aware of the bigger picture and how your brand fits in.

Become a Conscious Marketer.

But do so purposefully and cautiously...

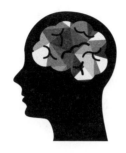

CHAPTER 13

dangerous territory

#FAIL

You have a choice to either be the disrupters or the disrupted.
—Steve Easterbrook, CEO of McDonald's

I CAN'T TELL YOU how many times I have heard people say that marketing is obvious. So easy. Piece of cake. 101.

Oh yeah? Don't tell my colleagues that!

If marketing is so obvious, then why do we see so many brands taking the wrong turn?

Why do we see so many brands put out marketing campaigns that go nowhere?

Why do we see so many brands offending a group of people and then apologizing for it?

Why do we see so many brands fall victim to disinformation with no proper response to it?

If marketing is so obvious, then why do we see so many brands #Fail?

If marketing is so obvious, then why do we see the role of CMO facing such turnover? The latest stat, to my read, is that the average tenure of a CMO is eighteen months. If marketing is so obvious, then why aren't more CMOs instantly successful and in their roles for years?

Why?

Because marketing isn't obvious, and not all marketers are entirely conscious all the time. Marketers get stuck in their own brand bubbles and lose sight of what's going on in the world around them. They get so caught up in the importance of their own brand that they forget that their brand might not be the most important thing in their consumers' lives.

Marketers often get tunnel vision and lose their consciousness. And when a brand has lost its consciousness, that's when there's likely to be a major #Fail.

We see it all the time. We read about it in the headlines constantly. We see it in our social feeds continually.

We say to ourselves, "How could they have done that?"

Because they weren't being conscious! And because it's just not all that obvious, especially when you're caught up in the middle of it.

Essentially, that's why agencies and agency relationships are so important. Agencies help brand managers stay objective and stay conscious of the bigger picture. Agencies have a broader view than just one brand and just one client, so they are likely to be more attuned to what's going on in the world.

But agencies #Fail too. All the time.

Marketing is just not that obvious, and all of us can lose our consciousness from time to time.

One of my first memories of a massive brand #Fail is from McDonald's. I love the brand, and I don't blame them, so please don't take this the wrong way if you work on the brand or if you're a fan too. Respectfully, the brand was really one of the first to embrace social media and use of the hashtag...sometimes there's danger when you're the first. While brands are all over social media now, McDonald's was one of the first brands in the Twitter space, using the social channel to connect with its consumers. So very conscious!

When you charter new territory, however, there are no rules in place. There are no best practices or lessons learned to draw upon. So you might very well stumble into some dangerous territory. It's not that obvious, after all.

McDonald's stumbled into dangerous territory.

To launch the brand's new wrap sandwich, McDonald's ran a promotion asking, "What's under your wrap?" New territory, but dangerous territory.

Sure, the brand got some postings of their sandwich wraps. Lots of fans embraced the intention of the promotion and gave some love back to the brand appropriately. But I'm sure you can also well imagine the other kinds of responses that the brand received from the question, "What's under your wrap?" Lots of pictures of things under wraps. Oh my! Dangerous territory.

How could they have done that?

History repeated itself again a short time later when McDonald's ran another promotion asking, "What's in store?" Once again, lots of fun postings of families enjoying the McDonald's restaurants, with lots of love from fans. But also lots of commentary about what people have found in store at McDonald's. Oh my! Dangerous territory.

How could they have done that?

Well, the truth is that McDonald's was a pioneer and continues to be one. The brand was one of the first in the space, so it couldn't have had the consciousness to know how it could potentially go wrong.

Now we are much more conscious.

Now we can look at these kinds of promotions in hindsight and say that it's all so obvious. It wasn't so obvious back then. And most of marketing isn't obvious now, either.

Not too long ago, there have been two major #Fails from two fashion retailers, shockingly happening back to back.

One was from H&M, which featured a black boy in an advertisement wearing a hoodie that said, "The cutest monkey in the jungle." Many people had problems with that. Dangerous territory.

How could they have done that?

Then another retailer, ASOS, featured a woman's choker that looked like a long belt. The brand name was Hanger. Many people had problems with that. Dangerous territory.

How could they have done that?

These two mishaps were relatively small in reach, and I doubt that anything was done purposefully. The brands just weren't conscious.

Marketing is a spectator sport; let's all learn from each other.

It's not always the brand marketing that gets brands in hot water.

We've seen CEOs speak out, seemingly without any consciousness, only to put the brand under fire. As we said, the

CEO is the voice of the brand, and sometimes that voice gets into dangerous territory as well.

Dolce & Gabbana's co-CEOs troubled people when they commented on in vitro fertilization. Dangerous territory.

Then there's Barilla, whose CEO upset pasta lovers worldwide when he declared that he didn't want gay people buying his pasta. Dangerous territory. The brand has spent years trying to recover its reputation, hiring industry experts to help. Only now is it starting to rebound.

Of course, many CEOs have gotten into trouble for things they never even said. Pepsi, for one, faced boycotts based on political statements attributed to the CEO but never stated by the CEO. Disinformation in action. *Marketing is a spectator sport; let's all learn from each other.*

Conscious or not, some of these types of behaviors do leave a lot of people asking, "Did they do that on purpose?"

I don't think so.

But you would think everything should be on purpose…

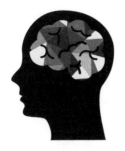

CHAPTER 14

running the organization

DO IT ON PURPOSE

They wouldn't call it work if it was easy.
—Jim's dad

SEVERAL YEARS AGO, A BOSS gave me a very important piece of advice without even realizing it. I was asking him what hadn't worked out with my predecessor, and he responded with a one-sentence answer that has stuck with me ever since:

"He didn't run the organization; the organization ran him."

At the time, it struck me as such a simple concept, so why would anyone not get it? How could you possibly "let the organization run you"?

Boy, was I in for a surprise.

The organization was in complete disarray at the time. There were no priorities, only deadlines. There were no plans, only fire drills. There was no order, only chaos.

It was no way to run an organization, yet everyone was running ragged.

My boss did me a huge favor in that one statement: he summed up what I needed to do in my first thirty, sixty, and ninety days.

Everything that I did and that the teams did had to be on purpose. Not necessarily with a purpose, but on purpose. Planned, organized, and on purpose.

I needed to prioritize the groups' work, I needed to put plans in place, and I needed to establish some order to the project flows and demands of the organization. Because my boss made that one statement to me, I didn't get caught up in the demands, deliverables, and drills that could have easily gotten me off to a bad start, just like my predecessor. If I hadn't paid attention to that piece of advice, I might have also gotten caught up on a runaway train and perhaps never gotten control of it.

I had to run the organization. My boss made me very conscious of that!

It's so important to not let the demands of the day run you around, constantly forcing your priorities and putting your plans on the back burner. If you let the fire drills take control, you'll never get ahead of the work enough to be able to run the organization. The organization will run you.

So adopt a few key measures to make sure that doesn't happen. Delegate to others. As a business leader, it's important to not get too caught up in the work. That's what the teams are for. Let your teams manage the details and the deadlines so that you can focus more on the big picture. You can be a consultant to the teams, for sure, but you don't have to do their work for them. Delegate!

Determine firm milestones. For key initiatives you are driving, it's important to determine firm milestones and stick to them. Don't let the demands of the day push back your timelines. Give project coordinators firm deadlines to meet and treat them like you'd treat any other business priority. Stick to them!

Dedicate time. Let's face it, the days and the weeks and the months can get away from us. Sometimes there's no avoiding the pressures of the moment. That's why it's so important to set aside time each day to do your own work—the work you need to do to run the organization. For me, the early morning hours are the best time for me to do my own work. And I always make time for some exercise, even if it means getting up earlier. Gym time is Jim time, and I'd recommend it for you too. But everyone is different, and everyone needs to find his or her own way. Find your own time!

None of this is easy. As my dad says, "They wouldn't call it work if it was easy."

But it's a lot harder if you have an organization that is running you, rather than the other way around. Heed the strong advice given to me back in the day, and you'll see your work produce results.

That's the best way to avoid a crisis...

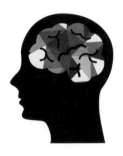

CHAPTER 15

crisis

STICK TO THE BRAND

There cannot be a crisis next week. My schedule is already full.
—Henry Kissinger, former United States Secretary of State

SO THE ORGANIZATION HAS run you ragged, and your brand has gotten a bit out of control? Now you've found yourself in the middle of a crisis. What do you do?

What would a Conscious Marketer do?

Stick to your brand! Control the solution to the crisis; don't let the crisis control you. Sound familiar?

Lots of experts have lots of advice for how to handle a brand that's in crisis. The one piece of advice we hear is, "Get out in front of the crisis."

"Control the message."

"Be transparent." Well, that one I would change to "be conscious." I'm sure you would have a guessed that one, though.

I have a slightly different take on that advice, particularly in light of what we've been discussing here. The biggest piece of advice that I give to clients in moments of panic is, "What's your experience?"

Or, in other words, "What's your brand all about?"

Including, "What are your values?"

And, "What is your voice?"

Also, "What else is going on in the world at the same time?"

Probably most importantly, "What do your consumers care about?"

All of these questions are about being conscious and are included in the question, "What's your experience?"

So when an airline company has a little puppy die on board because it was stored in the overhead storage bin, what does it do? Be conscious and stick to the brand!

So when a vegetable company finds out that its consumers are getting E. coli, what does it do? Be conscious and stick to the brand!

Like we've said, it sounds obvious. In theory, yes, but in the real world, it's often not so obvious.

During a crisis, we often panic and lose our senses. We forget what the brand's all about, and we forget what the brand stands for. We forget what's most important.

We lose our consciousness.

It's in that crisis mode, however, that we should remain at our calmest. We have to control the solution to the crisis, not have the crisis control us. We have to go back to the principles that make up our brand and recommunicate them.

We must stick to our brand in moments of crisis.

What do your consumers care about?

At the risk of talking about Starbucks too much, this is a company that consciously sticks to its brand during each of its crisis moments. The CEO instantly becomes the voice, and the CEO consciously takes responsibility, refers to the brand's values, and uses the brand's equity to form all steps moving forward.

Through the years we've seen many airlines control a crisis beautifully and we've recently seen some that don't control it at all. Those brands run out of control as a result.

We can all do that. If we've been conscious all along, it shouldn't be that hard. We know who we are as a brand, and we know our consumers. So go with that.

Easier said than done, I know.

But the more you know your consumers, then the easier it is...

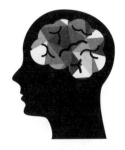

CHAPTER 16

isn't this just targeting?

ALIGNING WITH CONSUMERS

We regularly work with our media buying partners to ensure our ads do not appear on sites that aren't aligned with our values as a company.
—Kris Charles, spokesperson for Kellogg's

IT'S HUMAN NATURE TO assume that people do things on purpose. We say things on purpose. We react to things on purpose. We hurt each other on purpose.

On purpose.

When the many brand #Fail campaigns we discussed earlier happened in the moment, many people on social media assumed that it was done on purpose. They assumed that the brands or the CEOs did that or said that on purpose to get marketing attention.

"They did it on purpose."

I'm not sure that's always the case, but I'm not naive enough to just assume that it's not on purpose some of the time. In those various instances we will never know, unless the brand managers or CEOs come clean one day. I don't see that happening—at least not on purpose.

But I'm not convinced that it is all done on purpose. Why would any of us want to make that much of a public mistake? Just to get attention? C'mon, really good marketing gets positive attention, and that we do on purpose!

This is where Conscious Marketing really helps us make sure that what we do on purpose has purpose.

This chapter, if I'm doing my job, should remove all doubt in your mind about why you should think about being more conscious in your brand marketing. This chapter should also dispel a myth, or a preconceived notion, that holds some folks back from being Conscious Marketers.

Being a Conscious Marketer isn't about politics.

Say what?! That's right, I said it before.

Being a Conscious Marketer is not about forcing a stand on a social issue.

Huh? That's right, I said it before.

Being a Conscious Marketer is not just about giving back to the planet.

Really? That's right, I said it before.

Being a Conscious Marketer also is not just about acting responsibly.

Hey, what gives?

Well, yes, all of those perspectives can be parts of being conscious, for sure.

Being a Conscious Marketer is not singly what any of that is all about, although all of those elements can be a big part of it.

Ready? Really ready?

Conscious Marketing is all about targeting.

Targeting.

Being conscious: paying attention to politics, understanding social issues, contributing back, and acting responsibly are all exactly what you'd expect Conscious Marketing to be. But there's so much more from a marketing perspective. There's so much more to Conscious Marketing that is very much on purpose.

On purpose. Not having a purpose, although that's a part of it too. On purpose.

Being conscious is really about aligning the brand with its core target audience on multiple levels. And because politics, understanding social issues, giving back, and acting responsibly (among other things) is important to your consumers, then it has to be important to your brand as well. At least enough for you to be aware—enough for you to be conscious.

Being conscious aligns your brand with your consumers, and that's on purpose. It's all about targeting and alignment.

When Kellogg's pulled its advertising from the conservative news outlet Breitbart, the company wasn't making a liberal political statement (although many thought that was the purpose).

The brand was attempting to align with its consumer base and with their consumers' thoughts, feelings, and opinions. Kellogg's didn't feel the news organization's values and how it was expressing them (at the time led by lightning rod Steve Bannon) aligned with the company's values, which reflect the values of its consumers. Sure, instant backlash occurred, but the company stuck to its position, for its consumers. Kellogg's pulled out of Breitbart on purpose, for its consumers. Kellogg's is a Conscious Marketer.

Targeting. Kellogg's was targeting its core consumers. Its most loyal consumers. On purpose.

We can argue whether that was the right thing to do, but either way, it's targeting. I'll argue that purposeful targeting is always the right thing to do. Targeting is what marketing is all about. In this case, Conscious Marketing.

In an attempt to also target their own core consumers, many other brands followed Kellogg's move.

In a similar vein, Unilever announced that it will no longer support digital platforms that aren't actively fighting against "fake news." This wasn't a political statement aimed at the media or the current government administration. It was aimed at protecting Unilever's consumers. The company, and its brands, are consciously working to stop the spread of news that isn't accurate and that can be misleading. Those consumers who appreciate that will follow Unilever and its brands. Unilever is a Conscious Marketer.

Targeting. On purpose.

We can argue whether that was the right thing to do as well, but either way, it's targeting. Many other organizations followed Unilever's move, just like the case with Kellogg's and Breitbart.

By aligning on what's important to the target audience, brands are attempting to build deeper relationships beyond just the functional benefits of the product or service. By aligning with the target audience, the brand is showing that it cares and that it wants to support what's important to those consumers. By aligning with the target audience, the brand is being conscious and is marketing on purpose.

Gillette has famously targeted men who are looking to get and to be, "the best a man can get." The brand's target has guided its decisions to tackle social issues such as the evolving definition of masculinity and gender identity.

Targeting. Alignment. On purpose.

This is why it's important to understand that Conscious Marketing is really all about targeting: by aligning with the target audience, the brand is moving beyond being a product and becoming a brand.

An emotionally based brand…

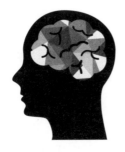

CHAPTER 17

becoming a brand

RISE ABOVE!

We see our customers as invited guests to a party, and we are the hosts. It's our job every day to make every important aspect of the customer experience a little bit better.
—Jeff Bezos, CEO of Amazon

THIS CHAPTER TAKES a page from my integrated marketing class at NYU, where we spend an entire semester dissecting the difference between products and brands. I can't possibly put fourteen extended classes into one chapter, but I'll try to give the important highlights.

The essence of the class: What is the difference between products and brands?

The quick answer to a very complicated question: the emotional benefit.

How's that for fourteen classes? I've got some explaining to do.

First of all, what are products? Products are simply a compilation of functional benefits. Products do things. Products fulfill specific needs. Products get stuff done.

Take skin care products, for example.

Skin care products cleanse, moisturize, and protect skin—all functional benefits. If truth be told, pretty much all skin care products offer those same functional benefits.

Sure, the manufacturers craft the messaging to make it sound like the benefits are unique, but in many ways, all products in the same skin care category basically perform in similar ways. Yes, there are certainly variations in packaging, fragrance, color, and even texture that may affect consumer choice, but essentially the product functions are identical.

Even if the products contain the newest, most advanced botanical extract complex multilayered bioengineered something extra special ingredient that no one else has…they still essentially do the same functional things. Apologies.

Consumers need products. We all need to cleanse, moisturize, and protect our skin. It probably doesn't matter much which brands we buy to get it done, from a functional perspective.

What's true with skin care products is most likely true in almost all other categories. Most products within any given category probably perform the same functional benefit—consumer brands as well as business products and services. My students generally agree!

It's just how it goes.

Brands, on the other hand, offer emotional benefits. Brands

Brands make consumers feel something special

go beyond just doing something. Brands make consumers feel something special.

This is very much true with skin care brands:

- L'Oréal: "Because you're worth it" (self-worth, self-esteem, accomplishment)
- Olay: "Fighting it every step of the way" (determination, fortitude, persistence)
- Clean & Clear & Under Control: "Taking control of skin that's out of control" (ability, strength, powerful)

(By the way, I wrote that Clean & Clear tag line back when I ran the brand, and it's still in use as the emotional benefit. Yeah!)

These skin care brands offer these emotional benefits to differentiate themselves from one brand to another. The emotional benefit is what draws consumers to brands because of how the brand makes them feel. So while the functional product benefits are all the same, brands try to own a unique emotional benefit different from that of any other brand in the category.

Consumers want brands. They want to feel something special. They most likely won't "feel" anything special from a product, so that's where the brand plays a role.

Consumers "need" products, but they "want" brands. Fourteen classes distilled down into seven words.

Allow me to continue to explain.

I might "need" a pair of yoga pants, but I "want" a pair from Lululemon. I might "need" a facial moisturizer to prevent wrinkles, but I "want" L'Oréal.

I might need a cup of coffee, but I want to go to Starbucks. Somebody else might want to go to Dunkin' Donuts. And someone else might want to use a Keurig at home.

While products do fulfill a need, consumers want to bring brands (not products) into their lives. Consumers want brands in their lives, above and beyond the functional benefits that the products offer.

For what is becoming more the norm than not, consumers are wanting those brands from Amazon. Or they are wanting Amazon more than the brands. Well, then again, Amazon is a brand—a lifestyle brand that has added incredible emotional value to people's lives.

Yes, that's a brand.

Consciousness makes the emotional benefit even more meaningful.

By being conscious, the brand proves to its consumers that it understands their lives. Being conscious shows that the brand's number one priority is the consumer, above and beyond just profits. Being conscious is what makes the brand relevant to its consumers.

Schweppes in Brazil understands that it needs to differentiate from its competitors with an emotional benefit. So, it did a study about sexual harassment in night clubs to raise awareness and ultimately help women feel safe. Very emotional and very conscious.

Being conscious enhances the emotional benefit and differentiates it even further. Being conscious makes consumers want the brand even more, more so than any other product available in the category.

Retailer REI proved this in honor of International Women's Day.

If you're not familiar with the brand, REI is a retailer specializing in clothing, gear, equipment, and accessories for outdoor activities. These items are available in a number of locations online and offline, and to be honest, the product offerings are not significantly different from that of other similar retailers. You can find a lot of the same items at Dick's Sporting Goods, for example.

But by talking to women about how the outdoors is a "level playing field" and that women shouldn't feel held back outdoors, REI is building an emotional connection for women to want to go to REI (instead of Dick's Sporting Goods). Complete with the hashtag #ForceOfNature, REI is telling women that everyone is equal outdoors, so don't let anything hold you back.

Perfect timing, I might add. Conscious timing.

As a result, while women may "need" outdoor equipment, they "want" to go to REI to get it.

REI is adding an emotional benefit to shopping for outdoor gear and apparel.

Amazon is also a retailer. Why do we sometimes feel like Amazon is taking over the world?

Sure, it's partly because the company offers a functional shopping benefit that far surpasses what has traditionally been offered by other online outlets. Service, pricing, shipping, returns, selection—all functional benefits. It's also partly because the company offers functional shopping benefits that far surpass traditional offline retailers as well.

But those aren't the reasons why it feels like Amazon is taking over the world. It's because the Amazon brand is making us feel something we don't feel from other retailers. Smart. Connected. Pioneering. Exploratory. Fulfilled.

So it's no wonder that Amazon can take that emotional connection and then advance into other areas, like shopping for entertainment. Online. Smart. Connected.

Amazon is conscious of how consumers want to shop (for everything in their lives) and how they want to consume products and services (for everything in their lives). Its entire range of products and services (including new areas not thought of before from a "retailer") makes consumers feel like they've explored all their options and found the best—over and over again, in a completely customized and satisfying experience that makes consumers feel like they've won.

Do other retailers make consumers feel that way?

As a successful marketer, consciousness will really uncover the unique emotional benefit that you can offer your consumers. Consciousness will raise you above just being a product and to being an emotionally based brand.

Conscious Marketing makes a brand.

REI and Amazon are great examples, but let's look at what really got it all going...

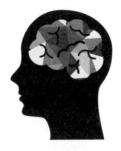

CHAPTER 18

the OGs of consciousness

COMPUTERS, CARDBOARD, COFFEE

It is not an economic decision to me. The lens in which we are making that decision is through the lens of our people. We employ over two hundred thousand people in this company, and we want to embrace diversity. Of all kinds.
—Howard Schultz, CEO of Starbucks

MANY BRANDS HAVE JUMPED on the Conscious Marketing bandwagon, that's for sure, and it's nearly becoming a cost of entry for marketers. For a brand to be fully engaged, it has to be fully and actively conscious. It's getting harder and harder to be successful in any other way.

Just like everyone took credit for teaching John Travolta how to dance for the movie *Saturday Night Fever* (Google it!), there are many brands that could take credit for making Conscious Marketing such a major movement. I'll never be able to give credit accurately to the exact brands (or people) that made it a revolution, but I would like to call out a few pioneers in the space.

Computers: IBM.

IBM is the OG (Google it!) in computing to my naked eye, but it's also an OG in consciousness, although a lot of it started on the inside of the company. IBM was one of the first big megabrands and megacorporations to be actively conscious about the makeup of its employee base and actively promoting its diversity. IBM publicly advertised its employee diversity not only as a way to retain and recruit talent but also as a way to elevate the brand. IBM formed internal support groups for women, who were under-represented in the industry (or almost any industry) at the time, and also for LGBT (before we added the "Q"), who were under-reported in the industry (or any industry) at the time. I remember seeing a print ad in a major publication (the name escapes me) with a group of employees who all self-identified as LGBT at IBM. I marveled at the bravery of coming out at work and the unprecedented support from the company. It was inspiring, consciously inspiring. Perhaps it was IBM's early consciousness that led the organization to its current innovations, like IBM Watson and AI.

Consciousness breeds success, that's for sure—IBM is a Conscious Marketer.

Cardboard: IKEA.

The OG in DIY (Google it!) home goods is also the OG in sustainability. From the company's inception, IKEA helped to define modern-day consciousness. I had the distinct honor of working on the global brand IKEA, and I witnessed firsthand its Conscious Marketing. Every single aspect of the IKEA business (including how the products, packaging, and shipping is conceived, constructed, and delivered) is done in a way that shows how IKEA is consciously aware of its impact on the environment. Consciousness is IKEA, and IKEA is consciousness, including a foundation that gives back to communities. IKEA started its business when it wasn't in vogue to broadcast sustainability efforts because it was seen as being boastful. But over time, the brand got more and more comfortable opening up about its conscious business principles. The more the company opened up, the more people wanted to know more and the more people associated IKEA with sustainability (even if they didn't call it that at the time).

The IKEA business grew as the generations responded to IKEA's unique offering. IKEA is a Conscious Marketer.

Coffee: Starbucks.

The OG in bringing coffeehouses to the masses is also the OG in taking a stand on social issues, thanks in large part to its OG CEO Howard Schultz. The Starbucks CEO was among the first to speak out about issues that concerned his consumers and his employees, like gun control, tax reform, gay marriage, education, and race relations. I'll never forget when he spoke at a shareholders' convention and basically told the audience (in not so many words) to sell their stock if they didn't believe in gay marriage ("gay marriage" was later repositioned as "marriage equality," thanks to some Conscious Marketing in and of itself). The company's statements often put the brand in hot water, but I believe that the CEO knew exactly what he was doing: targeting his consumers and protecting the interests of his employees.

The Starbucks brand is certainly not afraid to stand in the middle of an issue and is very aware (conscious) of its status in our popular culture all around the world. Starbucks is a Conscious Marketer.

I applaud these three early pioneers and the many others that were actively exhibiting consciousness at the time—early in time, or perhaps just in time—inspiring all of us to make consciousness an active part of our marketing today. Because they shared how they connected with their many constituents, others were able to follow in their footsteps.

What's your experience? Are you a conscious marketer?

Now it's time for you to share too...

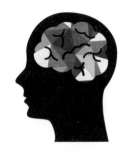

#tmwisc

THERE'S THAT WORD "EMPATHY" AGAIN

We want to stand a bit in this campaign for empathy, tolerance, and also the simple act of talking to one another, and if that happens over a beer, that's great as well.
—Nic Casey, marketing manager at Heineken

THOSE PIONEERS of Conscious Marketing knew something that many others didn't know at the time—that being conscious could positively affect their business.

Those CEOs, CMOs, brand managers, marketing directors, and communications directors (and presumably their teams) cared about the impact that their business had on people. They cared about how people perceived their business. They cared that what they were doing was connected to the wants and desires of their target audiences.

They cared about being conscious.

So now as you ponder and debate Conscious Marketing (because it is indeed a lively debate), regardless of your role with your brand, let me tell you why you should care.

#TMWISC: Tell Me Why I Should Care

Because they care. That's why.

You should care because these matters matter to your consumers, your shareholders, your employees, and your suppliers—all of your constituents and stakeholders, depending on the nature of your business and the business of your brand.

You should care because what matters to them should matter to you.

The more you understand that and embrace that, the more your brand will benefit from a more positive reputation, increased market share, better employee retention, improved talent recruitment, and eventually even better supplier relationships and competitive pricing. And perhaps even better relationships with your shareholders (public or private) via better share performance.

Any one of those benefits should be plenty for you to care about!

Take a look at the Heineken "Worlds Apart" campaign, where the brand brought people with wildly opposing points of view together to hash out their differences...over a beer. Over a Heineken beer. Emotional benefit: bringing people together to put aside their differences.

So conscious!

Heineken showed its consciousness by addressing an issue that is bothering a lot of its constituents: dealing with a divided world. By demonstrating how coming together to discuss our differences proves that we're really not that different at all,

Heineken became an active part of the solution. Heineken showed that it cares about the issues that its consumers care about, and it showed it cared enough to try to help. Over a beer, yes, but how many serious conversations have we all had over a drink? A cocktail? A coffee? A beer?

Heineken took it even further and encouraged its own employees to get together with people that they don't yet know, sharing a beer and discussing life's issues in the same thematic as "Worlds Apart."

Consumers and employees that share the same concerns... dealing with a divided world.

The "Worlds Apart" video got shared instantly.

Let's face it, sharing is the holy grail of social marketing. Sharing is also the holy grail of consciousness because that's how we start to understand each other better. We share points of view. That's how consumers and brands start to understand each other better too—they share points of view.

If you can get any of your constituents to share a positive experience with your brand, you will undoubtedly improve brand loyalty and reputation. They will be more conscious of your consciousness, and they will reward you by telling others.

So again...#TMWISC. What does all of this bring to you personally? Fame, a promotion, a career advancement? Yes. Job satisfaction? Yes indeed.

Any one of those benefits should be enough for you to care about.

But ultimately, consciousness brings us all empathy. I know I said this before, but it bears repeating, even at the risk of being repetitive.

I strongly believe that to succeed in today's world, you need empathy. It is a top determinant in personal success and

what matters to them should matter to you

in marketing success. We've already discussed its importance in marketing a brand. But what about in making a leader—a business leader?

#TMWISC

Empathy will make you more successful.

As business leaders, we must have empathy for our teammates as well. We have to understand what's going on in their lives and how their lives are affecting their work. Because no matter the person and no matter the situation, their lives are affecting their work. As a leader, you have to be conscious of that universal fact.

All of us, all of us, are going through something at any given time. While we might not talk about it at work, that doesn't mean it's not there and that it's not causing real impact.

Be conscious of that universal fact and show some empathy toward it.

If someone on your team seems a little less patient one day, let it go. If her normally perfect work product is a little less than perfect once in a while, then fix it for her. Give her a break! If she snaps at you and cuts you off multiple times in a row, roll with it.

Be conscious and show some empathy toward it.

Maybe someone else is going through something difficult and just can't live up to his own standards in that moment. Maybe there's something else going on in his world that is getting in the way of his work right now.

Maybe something else is up.

Be conscious and show some empathy toward it.

No need to say anything; no need to make it a big deal. Your teammates might not even notice—and perhaps that's exactly what they need right now. Perhaps they just need someone to let it slide this one time, someone to turn the other way and not make it a big deal.

That someone should be you.

Put yourself in your teammates' shoes and show them some understanding. Show them some empathy.

Think of your employees and teammates the same way we've been talking about consumers here: always put yourself in your consumers' position. In many ways, your employees and teammates are your consumers.

It may be a new way of operating for you, which means you, too, are growing. Be conscious of that as well, because your own personal growth is surely something you care about.

It may be just one part of some traditional thinking that you need to tear down…

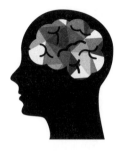

CHAPTER 20

are you still advertising?

THERE'S STILL A ROLE (PERIOD)

*When you hear "marketing," most people think advertising.
While we of course do that, we have made sure that
marketing has been redefined as innovation. We expect
our marketers to be the champions of "what's next."*
—Beth Comstock, vice chair of General Electric

THERE ARE MANY MARKETERS who claim that advertising is dead. Long live advertising!

Many of them have been saying that for years, ever since social media on the small screen took over our collective attention, drawing our eyes away from the big screen. Ever since "on-demand" television replaced "must-see" television. Ever since network programming started losing its hold to cable, which started losing its hold to subscription cable. Ever since *Sex and the City* became a phenomenon and you could watch each episode over and over and over again.

Ever since SJP became, well, SJP (Google it!).

All of those things, and a few others, have certainly changed advertising...but did it kill advertising?

Is advertising really dead?

Are brands still advertising?

What does that mean for advertising agencies?

Is Madison Avenue dead? Is there even a Madison Avenue anymore?

As Marvin Gaye would say, "What's going on?"

Like anything else in marketing, advertising has not died, but it has certainly shifted. It's broadened its definition. It's changed its course.

Advertising isn't dead. It's just changed. Drastically. Permanently. If history is any indication, it'll change again.

I was a brand manager at a time when the sixty-second television commercial ruled. Then the thirty-second commercial, and then the fifteen-second one. Now we're down to five seconds.

Five-second advertising!

Back in those days, circa late 1980s and early 1990s, we only really planned for television advertising, couponing, and retail displays to market our goods. Our marketing toolbox was somewhat limited. Little else in marketing moved the needle. When those things started to lose their effectiveness, we shifted our focus. Digital marketing and then social marketing and then content marketing came into favor.

Want to know the truth, though? It's all marketing. It's really all advertising.

It's all advertising, in the broadest sense of the word.

General Electric knows this all too well.

Sure, the company creates beautifully inspirational advertising that showcases GE's positive impact on people's lives all around the world. But that's not the only way that GE distributes its messaging, not by a long shot. GE uses the entire marketing mix, both B2C (business-to-consumer) and B2B (business-to-business) tactics to get both its product and brand benefits to its customers and the consuming public. In fact, if you listen to GE leadership, they will tell you that they consider their marketing not as advertising but as broadcast innovation.

For GE, advertising is marketing is innovation. I couldn't agree more.

It's all advertising, in the broadest sense of the word. In that context, advertising certainly isn't dead. Agencies of all types are still making advertising. It's just changed.

Some advertising is still of the thirty-second television variety, but so much more of it appears on so many other forms. So much of it isn't being created by advertising agencies. Digital agencies, social agencies, public relations agencies—they're all making advertising. Even advertising agencies are making advertising outside of their own traditional format.

Let's face it. Isn't this all really just advertising:

- Short-form ad that runs before an online video? Yes.
- Digital banner ad? Yes.
- Sponsored post? Yes.
- In-store display? Yes.
- Packaging? Yes.
- A piece of content distributed by an influencer? Yes.

It's all advertising. It's all marketing.

So while the traditional broadcast form of advertising may be losing its broad impact over time, other forms of marketing/advertising are replacing it. This is true of agency types as well. While the notion of a traditional advertising agency may lose its dominance, other forms are morphing to replace it:

- PR agencies that are becoming fully integrated across all media channels
- Digital agencies that are being fueled by strategy and creative
- Strategy agencies that are completing execution
- Consulting firms that are starting to implement their own strategic recommendations by doing "advertising"

It's all starting to blur, but it's all advertising, and it's definitely all marketing...just not how we may have traditionally labelled advertising (or even marketing, for that matter). So if you're in marketing of any sort, consider yourself to be in advertising. And if you traditionally viewed yourself as someone in advertising, then I would bet that you may need to change your definition of advertising. Same is true for public relations, digital, promotion, etc.

We all share this redefinition of advertising.

We all have to change how we describe and approach what we do now...

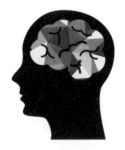

CHAPTER 21

two antiquated words

DIGITAL AND INTEGRATED

We should no longer be talking about "digital marketing" but marketing in a digital world.
—Keith Weed, chief marketing and communications officer at Unilever

IF YOU READ MY FIRST BOOK, then you know that I hate buzzwords.

While I know that they are unavoidable, and I even use one or two here and there myself, I just think buzzwords are a bad substitute for plain ole English (or your own native language). Just plain ole marketing language. I think people often use buzzwords to cover what they don't necessarily understand. No offense.

The funny thing about buzzwords is that they come and go, falling in and out of favor as a new one comes along and an old one falls by the wayside. In fact, it's not just buzzwords that come and go—marketing approaches and tactics fall in and out of favor as well. When one of them goes away, we need to learn to let it go. Let it go!

There are two such terms that I believe have become outdated, and using them now seems a bit old school and antiquated. When I hear someone say either one, I feel like he or she hasn't quite kept up with where marketing is going. Not trying to be judgmental, just progressive!

There are two words that I believe we should eliminate from our vocabulary.

The first term is "digital."

I don't think the word "digital" applies to marketing anymore. There was a time when email was just coming on board and websites were just starting to be formed, and "digital" was *the* buzzword being thrown around—way before "search" even became a concept.

Yes, there was life before Google, believe it or not.

Now, everything we do is "digital." Our lives are fully digital. Everything is on a screen: our food, travel, social activities, and even our banking. So how could marketing be anything but digital? Calling anything out as "digital" just doesn't make sense any more.

We need to be conscious of the fact that "digital" has lost its meaning.

The other antiquated word is "integrated."

"Integrated" always makes me chuckle a little inside when I hear it, and especially when I use it myself. Yes, I still use it, too, much to my chagrin. Even I have to keep telling myself that "integrated" and "integrated marketing" is a given these days and therefore shouldn't be called out as something special anymore.

Gone are the silos that once defined the various parts of a marketing plan. There is no more "advertising," and there is no more "digital," and there is no more "public relations." Integrated marketing is just marketing, and it includes all the ways we can connect with our target audience in a cohesive fashion.

We need to be conscious of the fact that "integrated" has lost its relevance because it's just what we do in marketing.

Oh shoot, I need to add one more word here that, when used, also makes us sound out of touch. I know I said two, but I have to throw in a third: "mobile."

"Mobile" has lost its meaning, too, much like "digital" and "integrated." Of course we are mobile, and in fact, we are mobile even when we are sitting at a desk or lying on a couch. We have a mobile device sitting in our hands (or in our bag or tucked in our pocket) pretty much all the time, whether we are moving or not.

In fact, "mobile" doesn't even mean "moving" anymore. So stop using it, just like you should stop using "digital" and "integrated." We can actually thank "mobile" for making those other two words extinct too.

We need to be conscious of the fact that "mobile" is just what we are now, and it has hence lost its meaning.

Unilever knows all too well the blurring of lines within marketing channels, with its beautifully crafted #SpeakBeautiful campaign from Dove.

The Dove campaign #SpeakBeautiful utilized Twitter's search technology to find language that was destructive to women's self-esteem and to automatically replace it with language of empowerment.

While the campaign played out on social media in an effort to change our social pop culture, it debuted via video format on the Academy Awards, which has become a massively influential pop culture beauty event. The video also streamed on all the brand's social channels. #SpeakBeautiful used multiple channels working together in an attempt to not only leverage our pop culture but change it as well.

We don't need a label that the campaign was digital or mobile or integrated, it was just a beatifully crafted conscious marketing effort!

Just take a look at how we shop and how that's all changed, eliminating the notion of digital, integrated, and mobile.

Many of us rarely step into a physical (brick-and-mortar) store anymore unless it's to pick up food or groceries. Many of us do our entire holiday shopping online (digital), and even much of that is on a phone (mobile). Black Friday (the day after Thanksgiving in the U.S.) has traditionally been the biggest brick-and-mortar shopping day of the year. This past year it was surpassed by a long shot by Cyber Monday (the biggest online shopping day of the year), just like in the prior year. But it wasn't just on Monday, and it wasn't just from a computer. People were shopping from all their devices, and in many cases (really for the first time), they were making purchases on their mobile phones while standing in a brick-and-mortar store.

Blurring of the lines and making our traditional marketing terms out of date and a bit out of touch!

Take a look at how we watch television.

Watching television is not just on a big screen, and it's not just at appointed times. We watch "television" on screens of all sizes, often on what might be called a "mobile" device, even when we are sitting at home. In fact, many times we are on multiple screens at home, watching and interacting all along the way.

Gone are the days of digital, integrated, and mobile.

Fortunately, there are two new words that we can quickly add to our vocabulary...

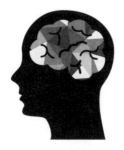

CHAPTER 22

two new words

OPINIONATED AND INCLUSIVE

For the first time, I felt like I was in a place where I understood other people, and they understood me.
—A developer at Microsoft

OUT WITH THE OLD, and in with the new!

While we are deleting "digital" and "integrated" and "mobile" from our marketing vocabulary, there are two new words that come along with being a Conscious Marketer. Add these words to how you think about marketing.

The first one is opinionated.

Being conscious means having an opinion and not being afraid to share it because you know it aligns with the values, behaviors, and attitudes of your brand and its constituents. Being a brand now means being actively conscious of what's happening in the world around your consumers and having an opinion about it. Of course you don't have to publicly state it or turn it into a confrontational debate, but as we've discussed consumers want brands to be opinionated and they want to know where a brand stands.

Being opinionated is no longer left for just people anymore. Knowing the opinions of your people, your consumers, is equally important now for brands too. Sharing those opinions with your consumers is where Conscious Marketing can be more effective.

The other word is inclusive.

While no brand can be all things to all people, we do need to be conscious of all people in our marketing. While no brand can pick all sides of an issue any longer, we do have to be conscious of those sides of an issue. Being conscious means understanding how people, your people, feel about issues, but it also means understanding the other sides of the equation as well. We have to be inclusive of all types of people, and we have to embrace diversity not only in the traditional forms— like color, ethnicity, sexual preference, etc.—but also diversity in thought as well.

As brands, and as people, we have to accept that there are varied points of view in the marketplace, and we have to include them in our consciousness. "Inclusive" is a new brand requirement now as well. "Inclusive" is another dimension of being a Conscious Marketer.

Allow me to digress here for a moment. "Inclusion" is a powerful word, but it's very different than the word "tolerance." I hate the word "tolerance." It's a bad word, and worse than any curse word in any language. As people and as marketers, we shouldn't "tolerate" anyone. "Tolerate" means we will put up with them and live with their differences. I don't want to "tolerate" anyone, and I don't want anyone to "tolerate" me. Nor do I want "acceptance" either. I want "inclusion."

Here's one example. Inclusiveness is why we are seeing major corporations like Microsoft, SAP, and Chase starting to consciously hire employees with autism because they recognize that these employees bring a different way of thinking and dedication to their work. So being opinionated and inclusive doesn't just apply to external communications; it also applies to internal policies around hiring, training, and support systems, which ultimately help to improve the products and services of the company. More to come on that for sure.

Microsoft went so far as to create special gaming devices for gamers who are physically challenged so that they can play equally with others.

These companies are not "tolerating" or "accepting" their diverse employee base. They are including everyone. Inclusive.

Okay, so I can't resist. I need to add one more new marketing word.

Persuasive.

Awareness used to be the goal of many marketing campaigns, which is why big broadcast media budgets were the norm and why advertising agencies ruled the marketing roost back in the day. Then it was all about influence (not awareness), which is why public relations campaigns and social media became an essential part of any marketing mix.

Now I believe it's all about persuasion.

To be a Conscious Marketer, brands need to be more persuasive in their messaging to convince people of the value they offer. It's the only way to stand out. It's not just about sending out messages or getting others to share them, but it's about getting consumers to embody them...to take them on and to insert the brand into their lives. The only way for a brand to do that is to be persuasive.

Persuasion can be tricky, however, because it can quickly appear to be disingenuous or forceful. So you need to be very conscious about how you approach persuasion. With the advent of digital marketing, we've seen persuasion come more often from a third party, not directly from the brand.

Hence, as one example, the birth of online product reviews. They've become not only influential in driving purchase intent but also persuasive in filling shopping carts.

Hence the rise of bloggers. Mommy bloggers, daddy bloggers, foodie bloggers, travel bloggers, fashion bloggers—there's a collection of bloggers, or influencers, in virtually every consumer category. These influencers have become very persuasive in their impact on brand marketing and their impact on driving sales.

Persuasion.

As Conscious Marketers, we need to be purposefully and authentically persuasive in our efforts. As well as being opinionated and inclusive.

But that all carries tremendous risk, right?

Not if you really know your consumer...

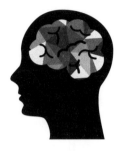

CHAPTER 23

knowing your consumer

ELEVATING THE EMOTION

Fashion is the armor to survive everyday life.
—Bill Cunningham, an American fashion photographer

IF I'VE SAID IT ONCE, then I've said it a thousand times: great marketing always starts with the consumer.

It's impossible to know too much about the consumer. It's impossible because the world, their world, is always changing and shifting and evolving. When you throw consciousness into the learning, then it becomes even harder to keep up because the range of knowledge that we require keeps expanding.

That's what's so exciting about marketing, and that's why I've stayed in it for thirty years now.

Complete and conscious knowledge of the consumer starts with what they need.

What are the functional benefits that your consumers need that you can offer?

Try to understand how those functional needs have changed over time, over their life stages, and over the generations. Generation X certainly has different needs from those of the baby boomers; baby boomers have very different needs from those of the generations that preceded them.

Once you have a good handle on what consumers need, then you need to learn what it is that they want.

As we've discussed, "wants" are different than "needs." "Needs" are functional, but "wants" are emotional.

The key is to elevate the emotional benefit to the next level, because you really know your consumer.

Allow me to explain.

As I confessed in my first book, I'm a Starbucks loyalist, and I admittedly talk about the brand too much. #Sorrynotsorry.

This may not sound odd to you at all until I also confess that I don't really like coffee. But admittedly, I do need a little boost in the morning to give me the spring in my step that I need to get to work.

As I highlighted earlier, I "need" a cup of coffee in the morning on my way to work. Truthfully, however, there are lots of options to get that cup of coffee. I literally pass dozens of options on my way to work, including making a cup of coffee at home with the Keurig machine that sits on my kitchen counter.

But I choose Starbucks on my way to work every single morning, no matter where I am in the world.

While I may "need" a cup of coffee in the morning (caffeine

"wants" are different than "needs."

boost), I "want" to go to Starbucks. Why? Let's take it to the next level.

It's the experience I feel there (a confident start to ease me into the priorities and stresses and deadlines and commitments and drama of the day).

"Wants" are much more important than "needs" because "wants" are much more differentiating. "Wants" are how you can hook the consumer into the brand. Of course you have to put this all into the context of how consumers live their lives.

For me, Starbucks must understand how coffee, its coffee, fits into their consumers' lives.

- How important are those product benefits to consumers functioning throughout their day?
- How important are those emotional feelings to consumers as they struggle with the many demands in their lives?

A caffeine boost is important to my morning routine for sure but getting mentally prepared for the many priorities on my to-do list for the day is quite another goal and is much more important—mentally and physically.

As brands, we must really understand both "needs" and "wants" if we are going to get the full impact of being a Conscious Marketer. We must understand "needs" and "wants" if we are going to have a successful brand proposition that's unlike any other in the category.

There's a very distinct place where all of this comes into play, and it's at the crux of marketing at its most powerful.

As you gather your ongoing information into the lives of your consumers, keep an eye out for the pain points in their lives because that's where you're most likely to make the biggest difference and add the most value. And fulfill the greatest emotion.

When you are able to relieve a pain point, then you are more likely to become a regular part of their lives.

Pain points live where the "wants" exist.

Getting me mentally prepared for the onslaught of activities for the day is a big pain point for me. Starbucks helps me prepare for it, and that's why I seek out the brand. That's a hell of a lot more than a caffeine boost.

Is it really performance at work that matters to me?

Or is it more about being successful to overcome the many naysayers through the years who have said that success would never happen for me.

Is that really what my day is about?

Is that really why it's so important to get a good start to every day? Is that why Starbucks is so important to me—because at the start of each day, the brand helps me to overcome the naysayers?

Whoa. That's another level!

That's a hell of a lot more than a caffeine boost. That's solving a pain point. That's elevating the emotion, and paying service to it.

Now couple that with the fact that Starbucks supports college education for all its employees, believes in marriage equality, and would like to contribute to solving racism in our society. I'm in.

Whoa.

That's a hell of a lot more than a caffeine boost. That's solving for multiple pain points consciously. That's elevating the emotion, and paying service to it!

I'm a Starbucks believer because I believe in the power of the Starbucks brand for me. For me.

There's a massive difference between "needing" a cup of coffee and "wanting" to prove those who didn't believe in me that they were all wrong. And "wanting" to align to a set of initiatives that I believe improve the world and how I want to contribute to it.

Too deep?

Never! You can never go too deep with an emotion.

Can you get this deep with your consumers' "wants"?

What are their "wants"?

How deep is the emotion?

What's your experience?

I maintain that you can get this deep in virtually any category, and no category is deeper than that of fashion. Fashion is the epitome of emotional benefits and the epitome of making a brand choice.

Think about it. While you might "need" a new dress for that high school reunion, why is it so important to "want" *that* dress? And *that* necklace? And *that* haircut?

There's an elevated emotional benefit in getting ready for that high school reunion that a relevant brand can tap.

Let me tell you, hair color isn't about covering up gray hair. Nor is adding highlights to give your color dimension. Nor is it making a fashion statement. Hair color isn't about confidence, either.

Hair color is about showing those kids who ignored you in high school that you are a player. You've got it going on.

Hair color is about negating those harsh comments you've heard that still stick with you today. It's about crushing that inner voice that says you're not good enough. Hair color is about who you want to be, despite the barriers you've overcome... despite all that you might be going through in the moment. When the brand that covers your hair also supports the issues that are important to you, then you have a deeper emotional connection.

Hair color solves pain points. The brand that nails that emotional connection will be a brand with consumer staying power. Hair color is a great example of elevating the emotion and making a deeper connection.

Holding a designer bag isn't about carrying your mobile phone and other essentials for the day. Nor is it about making a fashion statement.

A designer handbag is about showing the world that you've accomplished something for yourself. It's about showing up with your friends on equal footing, playing with them in the successes of life. Perhaps even showing up a bit better, if I can be so bold. It's about being the alpha of the group. A designer bag is about making it, not carrying it.

When the brand that carries your essentials also provides

the identity you want to show, then you have an elevated emotional connection.

Can you get this deep emotionally with your consumers?

Oh yes, you can!

What's your experience?

Maybe then, just then, you will have cracked what I consider to be the hardest part about marketing...

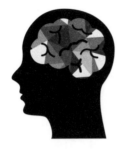

CHAPTER 24

conscious positioning

THE HARDEST PART OF MARKETING

A brand is a living entity—and it is enriched or undermined cumulatively over time, the product of a thousand small gestures.
—Michael Eisner, CEO of Disney

WHAT'S THE HARDEST PART about marketing?

Many would say coming up with enough money, but I have a very different answer: positioning. Marketing isn't about money—it's about positioning.

Positioning is the hardest concept in marketing to grasp, and I would argue that most brands don't do it very well...or at least there are many who could certainly do it a lot better.

Positioning is very hard. Especially if you have to create

positioning for your own brand. As someone who does it for many brands, even I still struggle with it to this day. Positioning is very hard. Doing for yourself for your own brand is even harder.

There have been countless books and articles written about the meaning of positioning and how to create one for brands. I've also seen dozens of definitions that point out the many intricacies of positioning and examine its importance. This is all well and good, but in many cases, these all confuse the true meaning of positioning and ultimately its role in marketing.

I like to keep things simple and in their simplest forms, so I'm going to define "positioning" as simply as I know how. Positioning is very hard, so the best way to really understand it is to keep it simple.

Positioning is the space you want to occupy in your consumers' minds when they think about you.

That's it. Keep it simple.

Positioning is the space you want to occupy in your consumers' minds when they think about you.

It's the space you want to occupy in your consumers' minds. That's it. It's that simple.

This "space" should be distinct and special, with no other brand in the same space.

Of course, then it's the marketer's job to get consumers to think about the brand! Inherently, that's not going to be all of the time but at certain times—certain times that will accomplish the brand's marketing objectives. That's when the marketing plan comes into play.

But a marketing plan isn't positioning. Nor is positioning any single piece of the marketing plan, like advertising, for example. And it's not simply a tagline, although a tagline should creatively articulate a brand's positioning.

Quite simply, at the risk of repeating myself, positioning is the space you want to occupy in your consumers' minds. Don't get more complicated than that, because actually that's quite complicated enough. Keep it simple.

So if you're Starbucks, to use my example from the last chapter, do you want me to think of your brand as coffee? Or as caffeine? Or as a quick pick-me-up?

No!

Those are functional benefits that any coffee or caffeinated beverage could also offer. Those are spaces that many products can occupy.

Elevate!

Functional benefits rarely create effective positioning. Positioning should inherently be emotional. It's the emotional benefit of your brand that should become the basis of your positioning.

Positioning—the space you want to occupy in your consumers' minds when they think about you.

Starbucks. That's the brand that makes me successful every day so I can prove all the naysayers wrong.

Yes! Positioning.

Starbucks is the "successful" space in my mind. It's the "prove them wrong" space in my mind. It's the "you can do it even though they say you can't" space in my mind.

Elevated emotional benefit!

Yes! That's positioning. Notice there's nothing in that space about coffee, or caffeine, or a quick pick-me-up. It's all emotional.

Disney has the quintessential positioning in my mind.

Is it a theme park?

A movie franchise?

A store?

A set of characters?

Yes!

But none of those are Disney's positioning. None of them.

Disney is a happy childhood and enduring childhood memories. That's the space that Disney occupies in its consumers' minds. Childhood either as a child, or reliving childhood as an adult, or providing childhood memories for your children. Happy childhood memories that are irreplaceable and unobtainable anywhere else other than at Disney.

Disney is happy childhood memories.

So how do you get to a place where you can figure out your positioning? You've got to really know what you can offer, and you've got to really know your consumer. And you've got to get deeply emotional.

So I'm sure you won't be surprised to hear me say that getting deeply emotional starts with being conscious of what's going on...

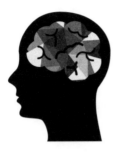

social listening

ACT LIKE A JOURNALIST

*I think the one lesson I have learned is that
there is no substitute for paying attention.*
—Diane Sawyer, journalist and television anchor

MARKET RESEARCH IS PERHAPS the most important step in becoming a Conscious Marketer.

All of us in marketing live and die by data, so you've got to become (if you're not already) living in a world guided by data. Data is the one thing that prevents us from just using our own opinion to make decisions.

That's right…don't use your own opinions to make decisions. Don't go there, ever. This so-called "mother-in-law" research can get your marketing off in completely the wrong direction.

You know the drill: "I asked my mother-in-law, and she likes the color blue." It's not important what your mother-in-law thinks or what you think. It's important to know what your consumers think, and the only way to do that is to do some market research.

For Conscious Marketing, I'd recommend looking at three distinct dimensions of research to get a full picture of what's going on in consumers' hearts and minds.

Research in three ways: consumer, brand, and cultural research.

Consumer Research.

Go deep into the lives of consumers and suss out what's most important to them. Understand how they go about their days and find out what keeps them "up at night," as they say. Discover their stresses and see how they cope with them. Follow how they prioritize the many demands they face and how they get things done. Don't just look at the demographics (facts and figures), but also look at the psychographics (thoughts, feelings, attitudes, behaviors).

Brand Research.

It's also important to find out how consumers feel about the brand right now as well. What do the reviewers say? What's the current sentiment about the brand? I would actually do a SWOT analysis of how consumers view the brand by analyzing the brand's:

- Strengths: What's good about the brand?
- Weaknesses: How could the brand be better?
- Opportunities: Where could the brand go that it hasn't been yet?
- Threats: What could stand in the way of the brand's success?

Look at all of this from the consumer's point of view, not your own. We tend to think more highly of our own brand than what is likely to be reality. Look honestly and objectively at how consumers view the brand. It'll be eye opening and a learning experience—I can guarantee that. But only if you're completely objective.

Cultural Research.

This is where consciousness kicks in. Make sure you know what's going on in the world around your consumer:

- What are the prevailing social issues that occupy their minds?
- What's the political climate that affects their lives?
- How do they feel about the issues that worry them the most?

As we've discussed, you don't necessarily have to weigh in on any of these factors but understanding how consumers view them is paramount to being conscious.

If it's important to them, then it should be important to you too.

What's the best way to get all this information? There are lots of ways, actually, and people have written entire series of books on market research best practices. I'm not going to tackle that, but I will tell you one cheap and easy way to learn about consumers that is right at your fingertips: social media.

IMHO, social media is one of the best ways for any brand to learn about its consumers. It's basically free, and you can access the information 24/7 whether you're a big blockbuster brand or a small business owner.

Most marketing people think that market research is time-consuming and cost prohibitive. It certainly can be. Custom research requires a big commitment. But custom research isn't the only way to learn about consumers, their perceptions of the brand, and what's going on in the culture.

Social media.

Check out the social media channels of your consumers, and you'll see what's what and who's who in their lives. It's all there in a picture, a post, a video, a link, and especially a hashtag. Your consumers are easily searchable by any key demographic or any given key topic.

You just have to dig into it all...dig into social media, and act like a journalist.

Act like a journalist who's writing a piece on your consumers and what's important to them. Be an open book and an open mind, looking to objectively profile what they're all about. A journalist leaves no stone unturned, so neither should you. While a journalist may go into research with a likely hypothesis, there's always the possibility of data sending the thinking in another direction. While looking for one nugget of information, a journalist often finds another that points to a new way of thinking.

That's the beauty of journalism and of market research as well. A journalist would never use one source, and neither should you. And remember that a journalist is always completely objective. No judgments, no personal opinions, and certainly no disinformation.

You should also follow those who influence your consumers and those who are persuasive in their decision-making—not just celebrities but bloggers and media personalities who post and discuss what's important to your consumers.

As we've discussed, there are bloggers for just about any

passion. Follow them! In fact, follow the journalists who cover the issues that are important to your consumers as well. They are a wealth of deep and spirited information.

This is all free, by the way. It just requires some time and a commitment to continually learn.

There are also many sources of industry reports that you can subscribe to that will provide a daily, monthly, quarterly, or yearly take on virtually any industry or target audience you can imagine. These are often written very well by journalists and industry analysts who spend their professional lives getting to know key industries. While some require a bit of an investment, most aren't that expensive, and they'll give you an objective take on the industry and the consumers who buy in to it. You might even get a glimpse into some perceptions of your brand as well.

But most importantly, please do one thing the entire time you are looking at market research: listen.

Most of us just aren't good listeners, and I'm self-aware enough to know that about myself, too. I'm conscious that it can be my own issue at times.

Listen.

While we should be listening, most of us are thinking about how we are going to respond when the other person finishes talking. We are thinking about ourselves rather than listening to others. Or, we are thinking about our own opinions instead of just absorbing. That doesn't work when it comes to Conscious Marketing. Conscious Marketing means active, conscious listening, and truthfully, none of us are the best we can be at it.

The market research we just discussed is in fact just that— listening.

Listen!

So this is my plea for you to spend more time consciously listening.

We tend to focus squarely on our own brand, thinking about ourselves most of the time. But our consumers don't spend all of their time thinking about our brand, so we shouldn't either.

We should be thinking more about them than we do about ourselves. If we spent even just a little more time listening to our consumers, then we'd know them a lot better.

Listen!

So yes, this means you have to be monitoring all day long, every day. You should be monitoring what's going on in the world and monitoring how your consumers are responding to it.

Active monitoring is an active part of listening, which is an active part of being conscious. Let's face it: if you're like me, you're probably doing this anyway. I read my news feed all day long because the news changes all day long. I'm also on my own social channels, too, staying connected to friends and colleagues around the world. I'd like to suggest that we all spend just as much time following and monitoring our consumers as we do our networks. It'll pay dividends for our brands.

Part of your monitoring should include brand sites, including your own and your competitors' sites. Consumers actively post their thoughts on brand marketing right on brand channels just as much as anywhere else. It's important to actively monitor those comments and respond to them, especially the negative ones. In fact, the true test of consciousness is exactly how you respond to negative comments about your own brand. I'd recommend you be honest, transparent, and conscious.

Listen!

Ultimately, listening forms the emotional connection you need to become a brand...

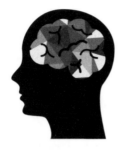

CHAPTER 26

pioneers in emotion

THE ABCS

When dealing with people, remember you are not dealing with creatures of logic, but with creatures of emotion.
—Dale Carnegie, founder of Dale Carnegie Training

WE TALKED ABOUT the difference between a "need" and a "want," and how a "want" is essentially the basis for being a brand. If you can't satisfy a "want," you not only won't have a sale, but you also won't really have a brand. And without an emotional connection, you can't satisfy a "want."

It's simple as that.

Creating an emotional connection is not a new concept.

Brands were founded on emotional benefits from the very start, because people are founded on emotions.

Think about the relationships you have in your life. They're all based, for good or for bad, on emotions. We're not really in a relationship with someone because of a functional benefit. We are creatures of emotion. Thank you, Dale Carnegie. Google it!

Brands are creatures of emotion, too, if you get the emotion correct.

I'd like to salute a few pioneers who really did it right, right from the start. The ABCs of emotion, if you will.

A is for *automotive*.

Purchasing a car is a big decision, and it generally starts with a lot of research. Consumers consider all the facts and make all their product comparisons well in advance of the actual purchase date. Product features play a big role in identifying the car to buy, but buying a car is ultimately an emotional decision. As is true in virtually every category, the product features are generally the same. Cars all provide roughly the same function, or certainly cars within the same subsegment provide roughly the same function. So making a car purchase comes down to an emotional connection with the brand rather than with the leather seats or the cool steering wheel or the sound system. All cars have those in one sense or another.

Think about the brands in the automotive space.

Choosing, let's say, a BMW or a Mercedes is mostly an emotional process. BMW is "The Ultimate Driving Machine." Mercedes is "The Best or Nothing."

Both brands, at the end of the day, are ultimately a "want." But BMW and Mercedes aren't the only cars with emotional benefits. No car has done a better job of creating an emotional connection than the brand Volvo.

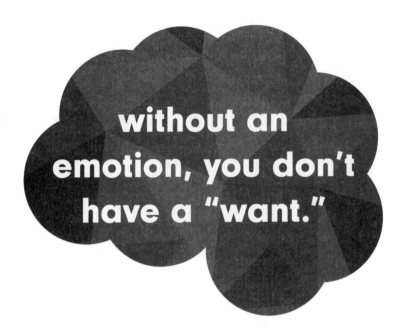

without an emotion, you don't have a "want."

Volvo is synonymous with safety, but the emotional connection goes deeper than that. A few years ago, the company declared its mission: "No one will be killed or critically injured by a new Volvo by 2020." Wow, that's taking both product and brand serious! If you buy in to safety, real safety, and a "guarantee" of safety as a real necessity, then you're going to "want" to get a Volvo.

B is for beauty.

The beauty category (hair care, skin care, color cosmetics, etc.) is right up there with automotive when it comes to brands making an emotional connection. Choosing a beauty brand is literally all emotion since (once again) all the products basically perform the same functional benefits. Cleanse, moisturize, treat, cover gray hair, etc. So brands rely on emotion to differentiate.

There's no better brand than the original L'Oréal. "Because You're Worth It." Best emotion ever created in the category and one that the brand has stuck with for decades. Self-worth is definitely a "want." Perhaps even a universal want, hence the tremendous success of the brand.

L'Oreal's emotional benefit of "self-worth" is different than the emotional benefit of "confidence," which is a word we often hear, too often, in marketing. We talk about it all the time in my NYU class.

"Confidence" is a generic. Virtually every brand can, and often does, promise confidence. It's not differentiating to say a brand builds confidence. In some ways, they all do.

Go deeper!

C is for *colas*.

Sure, beverages provide functional benefits. They quench thirst. Wake us up. Refresh on a hot day. But the brand Coca-Cola is far more than just those functional benefits. Coca-Cola is "happiness," the original "happy" brand! Note the exclamation point!

Long, long ago, Coca-Cola spoke about harmony and happiness. In 1971, on a hilltop in Italy, the brand filmed the now infamous, "I'd Like to Teach the World to Sing." "Open Happiness" has been the brand's call to action ever since. Coca-Cola is all emotion, which is what makes it one of the most powerful and most successful brands in the world.

"I'd like to buy the world a Coke." I'd like to have any brand I work on have an equally powerful emotional connection as Coca-Cola!

Other beverage brands have not been able to capture this same level of emotional connection, which is why Coca-Cola is such a classic (pun intended for those who've been around long enough to know). Google it!

The brand Vicks attempted to not only build an emotional

connection but do it in a conscious way with #TouchofCare. By featuring a transgender woman in India who adopted her daughter, Vicks was able to show that family is caring.

Now you do the same...what's your emotional connection? What's your experience?

It's as simple as that. Yeah right! You just have to make sure it fits your brand.

Oh yes, then there's that...

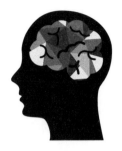

CHAPTER 27

keep it real

CONSISTENCY IS JUST AS IMPORTANT

Barbie is a great example of how we've taken a really important step forward in focusing not on what Barbie is as a toy but what Barbie enables through the power of imaginative play.
—Juliana Chugg, executive VP, chief branding officer of Mattel

THIS CHAPTER IS GOING to be a lesson in consistency, something that is a hallmark of great marketing but rarely practiced, as odd as that may seem.

Let's be real...Conscious Marketing has had its fair share of failures and controversy. We've spoke about a few of them. And while there may be many reasons for each and every one of them, I'd say there really are two factors that can cause a #Fail in being conscious.

Two reasons, if you will, why a brand wouldn't get the effect it is hoping for.

Most of the time, #Fail happens in Conscious Marketing because the brand isn't conscious enough. There's often a #Fail when the brand doesn't do its homework and doesn't fully understand the dynamics around a given issue. There's often a #Fail when a brand assumed it could simply put something out there and that it would be appropriately understood.

We see it quite a bit.

McDonald's "What's Under Your Wrap" is a good example, and we discussed it in Chapter 13. Another example is Heineken showing a range of ethnicities and skin colors in a video campaign but unconsciously using the tag line, "Sometimes, Lighter Is Better." Ouch.

McDonald's and Heineken assumed that its messaging would be understood, which is an all-too-common #Fail.

There's another reason why we see a #Fail from time to time. Something even more fundamental to being conscious and to being a Conscious Marketer.

Inconsistency. Many brands just aren't consistent with their Conscious Marketing.

Sometimes brands can try to be conscious, but it ends up being inconsistent with the rest of its marketing. So the consciousness comes off as insincere, inauthentic, and perhaps not appropriately having a role in the conversation at all.

Brands can #Fail when their Conscious Marketing isn't consistent with the brand.

Which is why you have to be so careful when voicing an opinion or taking a stand or even supporting an issue. You have to make sure that it is entirely consistent with every other aspect of your brand and that it is central to what your brand itself stands for.

When it's consistent, it's marketing at its best.

Here's a great example: Gerber (as in the baby food) just recently announced its latest "spokesbaby." Over 140,000 babies entered the contest to be the new face of Gerber, and little Lucas won because of his "expressiveness" and his "winning smile." Lucas also happens to have Down syndrome—a first for the brand.

Gerber made a conscious decision to pick a baby with Down syndrome to make a point: "Every Baby Is a Gerber Baby." Picking Lucas was not only very conscious of what parents are feeling now, but it was also entirely consistent with Gerber's brand equity. Celebrating all babies.

Consistency.

Barbie is another brand that consistently makes conscious decisions in its marketing. The brand's recent product line celebrating historical women in science to promote careers in STEM (science, technology, engineering, mathematics) was incredibly conscious and consistent—just like the brand has been for years, celebrating the many career options for women (and men).

The brand also featured a boy playing with the new Barbie Moschino designer collection in a recent campaign. Barbie showed a conscious understanding that its consumers aren't just girls...something consistent with the rest of the brand's marketing.

But when the brand isn't behaving consistently, it's readily apparent right away.

Just like when RAM trucks used a quote from Martin Luther King, Jr. in its Super Bowl advertising. In the spot, Martin Luther

King, Jr.'s voice came out of nowhere with no linkage to the RAM brand, its messaging, or its own history.

It left the impression that the brand was using Martin Luther King, Jr.'s voice just to grab attention, with no apparent greater purpose. People were left scratching their heads and questioning the validity of the RAM brand. Using Martin Luther King, Jr. as a voice-over was inconsistent with the rest of the RAM brand's marketing. Consumers spotted it in a New York minute and called it out immediately.

It's hard work being a Conscious Marketer. You have to carefully consider every move, making sure each move is consistent with the next.

So make sure that the brand's consciousness is real and consistent, in addition to being relevant. Make sure the consciousness fits with what the brand stands for and how you've positioned the brand in the marketplace. And make sure that it's always important and relevant to the consumer, each and every time.

Because without that linkage, you've got no impact and no real and relevant consciousness.

I know that none of this is very easy.

In fact, it's getting a little tense...

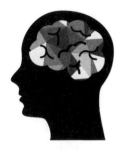

CHAPTER 28

feeling tense

FIND THE PAIN POINT

Whether you are a global brand or a smaller brand that's just getting started, the rules still apply: you have to make me feel something.
—Matthew Luhn, an American writer and story consultant at Pixar

"WHERE'S THE TENSION?"

"Where's the tension?"

"Where's the tension?"

I can't tell you how many times I've heard "creatives" ask that question! I've heard it so many times that I now ask it myself. I know how to follow smart people. What I once thought was a high-and-mighty phrase is actually a stroke of genius.

Of course, I've tailored that to, "What's your experience?"

But you first have to know the tension. In many ways, "Where's the tension?" leads you to "What's your experience?"

What exactly is "tension"? What is "tension" in the context of Conscious Marketing?

Earlier we spoke about pain points. Pain points are where consumers have a "want."

Understanding consumers, determining the "want," and finding a pain point is half the battle. We have to win the war, and that win comes from giving consumers some relief for those pain points.

Relief can be from a product standpoint, like quenching a thirst or satisfying a hunger. But relief can also be from an emotional perspective, like in terms of getting consumers ready to take on their day or giving them back the vitality they once had when they were younger. And the real win comes when you provide both functional and emotional relief.

Where there is a pain point, there is also tension, and where there is tension, a brand can provide relief. Both functionally and emotionally.

The key is to find the tension where you can give relief from both a product and a brand standpoint. The relief has to come from both perspectives. When you do it consciously, then you truly have a win for everyone involved.

Think of it like you are writing a story. Or a great movie.

I thought I'd give you three examples that all reside within the feminine hygiene category—a category that has both functional and emotional benefits like any other, but perhaps with higher tension than many. And they all three make for great stories.

First up is the brand Always, with its now infamous #LikeAGirl campaign.

The brand Always found the tension when its research showed that a girl's self-confidence plummets when she reaches puberty. Always, as a brand, becomes a relevant product right when a girl hits puberty too. So the brand created a campaign to boost girls' self-confidence right at a time when they need it most, with a product that helps them physically right when they need it for the first time. The brand Always found the tension and relieved it.

Then there's the brand Flo Starter Kit, a start-up in the feminine hygiene space that offers starter kits to young girls who are facing their first period.

The brand tackles the peer pressure that comes from developing as a woman and the role of mom as a guide during this trying time in life. The pressures of puberty play out differently here than in Always, but the brand relieves tension nonetheless as each girl "finally" gets her turn and is able to draw upon the starter kit to tackle this very dramatic first moment in life. The brand Flo Starter Kit found the tension, a different kind of tension, and relieved it.

On the other end of the spectrum is the brand BodyForm, a UK-based company in the feminine hygiene category as well.

This brand voice mocks the typical advertising in the feminine hygiene category and it strikes an emotional chord with women at a time when they are least in the mood, shall we say. By acknowledging that there's nothing to love or celebrate about a period, the brand was able to solve a tension around the conflicting feelings about being a woman during a period. The brand BodyForm found the tension, a different kind of tension, and relieved it, both emotionally with its campaign and physically with its products.

Three brands, three tensions, but with essentially all the same product—proving that you can create an emotional connection with a target audience, based on their specific pain points and tensions…and your brand's unique ability to provide relief.

Let's do one more example. Vans, as in the skateboarding shoe, has been supporting women and young girls around the world in learning how to skateboard. In some parts of the world, girls aren't allowed to skateboard. So the brand partnered with the women's organization Girls Skate India to inspire young women to learn to skateboard and then conducted skateboarding clinics to teach them. Plus, of course, Vans supplies the best shoes to skateboard.

Vans found the tension and relieved it.

Of course, if you notice, these stories of finding the tension and relieving it all make for great storytelling. And with great storytelling, you have the ability to connect both functionally and emotionally. Add in some consciousness, and you have marketing gold.

The key is to find the tension to solve, consciously…

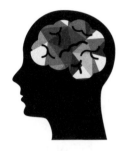

CHAPTER 29

finding your tension

WHAT, HOW, WHERE?

I also bring a compact umbrella. When I pack an umbrella, it doesn't rain.
—Jerome Griffith, CEO of TUMI

FINDING THE PAIN POINT, understanding the tension, and then providing relief is key to being a Conscious Marketer.

So it's about time, if you haven't already done so, to find your consumer's pain point, to identify the tension, and to provide relief. I know it sounds like we're talking about health care, but this applies to every category!

Give it a try, if you haven't already.

The secret comes in uncovering where these three things intersect—what, how, and where:

- *What* is the problem you can solve for the consumer?
- *How* can your brand uniquely solve it, functionally and emotionally?
- *Where* does this fit within the greater context of what's going on in the consumer's life?

WHAT:

We wouldn't buy products if they didn't solve our problems.

TUMI (as in the luggage brand) has had a huge resurgence in the past few years because it solves a problem: packing a wide range of clothing, accessories, and work items for business travel. What problem do you solve?

HOW:

We wouldn't consider products if we didn't understand how they will solve our problems.

Despite the many options out there, unlike any other brand, TUMI offers the complete suite of packing options for business travelers who want to look like they're put together and successful. Business travelers have a lot to carry from city to city, and there's a range of clothing occasions to cover on a typical business trip. It's very hard to pack it all, and we all often end up leaving something important behind. Been there, done that. With its hanging suit bags, tech pouches, and carry-

What problem do you solve?

on backpacks (among other items), TUMI solves that problem for any business traveler.

How do you solve your consumers' problem?

WHERE:

We wouldn't want a brand unless it relieved the tension we are feeling.

TUMI understands that it's a competitive job market out there and business travelers have to look the part despite the stress of travel, the feeling of job insecurity, and the time away from home and family. TUMI understands all of that and helps business travelers look organized, successful, youthful, and accomplished. TUMI solves the tension by helping business travelers look stylish yet at the same time helping them travel efficiently.

How do you relieve your consumers' tension?

Marketing Campaign:

When you look at the marketing campaigns from TUMI, you'll see where it solves this tension. Everything is organized, from soup to nuts from a business perspective. But the travelers look on the top of their game, seemingly ready to handle anything that comes along.

Product Lines:

Bags of every size, shape, and form, for any wardrobe combination. Even packing cubes to organize the essentials that then fit into any bag.

Retail Outlets:

TUMI products are right where you need them, right at the airport (among other places).

Influencer Endorsements:

TUMI tells motivational stories of road warriors who have achieved great success, with TUMI keeping them organized and moving.

Style Collaborations:

The TUMI universal style mixes well with others for a unique look, like the tropical collaboration with Orlebar Brown.

Giving Back:

TUMI supports childhood cancer research by supporting St. Jude Children's Research Hospital, because many business travelers have children and miss them most when they're not at home.

Going Global:

While TUMI may have started in the United States, it's available globally and conveniently for business travelers worldwide, both domestically and internationally, whether you're in your home country or abroad.

TUMI is a Conscious Marketer. TUMI understands where the tension exists for its consumers and solves for it, time and time again.

What's your experience?

Try to figure out your what, how, and where, and you'll be on the way to being a Conscious Marketer too.

Note that there's a lot more to the "where" part of the equation...

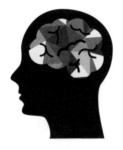

a note about touchpoints

NO MORE ADVERTISING

You should make decisions with consumers in mind,
always trying to imagine how they would react.
—Carlos Brito, CEO of Anheuser-Busch InBev

IN MY FIRST BOOK, *The Experience Effect*, I spent a lot of time talking about touchpoints. I'm not going to do that in this book because here we are talking more about being conscious. But, of course, I do still have a few things to say!

The entire notion around *The Experience Effect* is that a brand must be consistent in its messaging across all touchpoints if it wants to create a seamless brand experience that drives loyalty. But a cookie-cutter approach won't work anymore, either. The brand must maximize each touchpoint for its best role in the total brand experience.

In essence, touchpoints should move consumers along a journey of your brand experience, relating to them on a very conscious level at each point.

As Conscious Marketers, we will keep that approach intact but add the important element of consciousness to the equation. And when thinking about being conscious, we should also consider a few important things when choosing those touchpoints.

For example, I'm not sure that traditional advertising plays such an important role anymore. We discussed earlier about how virtually everything is advertising, but here I'm specifically speaking to broadcast television advertising. Network or broadcast advertising has typically been a one-way dialogue, which isn't necessarily being so conscious. Sure, you can push out a message of consciousness as part of being a Conscious Marketer, but the brand has to do a lot more than that.

The brand has to solve a problem—find a pain point and relieve the tension. That's probably not going to happen in advertising. Traditional advertising can contribute, but alone it's not enough.

I think of the work that Stella Artois is doing to provide clean drinking water to those in need around the world. "Buy the Lady a Drink" is a great way of giving back to the community and involving consumers at the same time.

For every iconic Stella Arbis glass or chalice purchased, drinking water is provided to communities that don't have access. And while the brand does use advertising and a celebrity (Matt Damon) to raise awareness for the program, it relies on many other touchpoints to actually deliver a mechanism to participate in the program—like its website and social channels. And the social influencers the brand leverages to spread the message and drive participation. And the retail outlets that actually carry the glasses.

These other touchpoints, in my view, are more effective in connecting consumers to help solve the problem of access to clean drinking water. But if you notice, no one touchpoint does all the marketing work. The flow of communication from one touchpoint to another is what will ensure the program's success.

As a manufacturer and global consumer of drinking water for its own beer production, it makes sense for Stella Artois to be leading this particular cause. Pain point, tension, relief…in a conscious way and along various touchpoints working together to engage consumers.

Here's an idea that you may second guess: Consider using your competitors as touchpoints too!

Have I lost my mind?

No! Increasingly we are seeing traditional competitors within a category start to work together to accomplish goals. Skyy Vodka and Absolut Vodka recently united to support marriage equality in Australia. Burger King supports McDonald's childhood cancer fundraising efforts in Argentina, giving both brands accolades.

So my point here is that you should shift your thinking on touchpoints away from general advertising to raise awareness and more toward touchpoints that drive very conscious participation from the consumers you are trying to activate.

But don't make them work too hard…

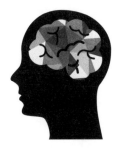

don't make them work

DITCH THE BOX

*There is only one boss: The Customer. And he can fire
everybody in the company from the chairman on down,
simply by spending his money somewhere else.*
—Sam Walton, founder of Walmart

IN THE LAST CHAPTER, we discussed "Buy the Lady a Drink"
from Stella Artois, a great example of relevant consciousness
and a total brand experience. What's not to love?

But there's one thing I do want to say about that particular
example. In some ways we've moved beyond this kind of
Conscious Marketing. Now I love what Stella did, or I wouldn't
have included it in my book, but there's a piece of "Buy the

Lady a Drink" that we as marketers have evolved away from in many cases.

We shouldn't make our consumers work for our Conscious Marketing. We shouldn't make consumers do the heavy lifting so that we can fulfill on our own brand consciousness.

We should do the work, not the consumers.

In the case of Stella Artois, the brand makes consumers do the work. In order for the brand to help supply drinking water to those in need, consumers have to buy a glass from the brand. In this case, a branded chalice. "Buy the Lady a Drink" puts consumers to work instead of the brand.

Still a great program, but it requires consumer action to make it happen. I believe that for the most part, we've moved away from making consumers do all the work. Although, again, I do love the campaign. Just making a point!

You know the drill: the "donation box" at the retail cash register, asking for consumers to donate extra change or a buck or two to the retailer's cause as consumers go through the checkout line. Or when the cashier, at the end of the transaction, asks if you'd like to add one dollar to your bill to support the brand's charity.

It's all well and good, but honestly, the brand should be doing the heavy lifting, not the consumer.

Don't make the consumer work for your consciousness.

Now I'm not talking about the TOMS shoes "buy one, give one" business model, because the brand is still doing the actual donating to charity. I'm referencing when a brand simply asks for the consumer to do all of the work. With few exceptions, this is not consciousness that works anymore. At least not for me.

Take a look at Walmart. It has publicly stated that it is working toward the goal of 100 percent renewable energy and zero waste in its operations and supply chain. That's the brand working toward its own consciousness, not asking the consumer to do anything except buy into it. Walmart understands that consumers have a choice, and the company is hoping that by being more conscious of its impact on the world, it can strengthen consumers' respect for the brand and persuade them to choose Walmart more often. Walmart is being a Conscious Marketer.

Consumers want to know what *you* are doing to contribute to the community, not what you are asking *them* to do. It doesn't work. It's not conscious, and it doesn't have the effect that it once had.

The sister brand to Stella Artois, Budweiser, made a commitment in the U.S. to only use renewable energy. That works!

And this one works…

Burger King in Argentina took a bold position and directed its customers to go to McDonald's one particular day to support McDonald's "McHappy Day," when all sales of Big Macs are donated to help children with cancer. Burger King didn't want to take away from the charity effort, so it stopped selling Whoppers on that day and promoted sales of Big Macs (its competitor) instead. Both brands are Conscious Marketers. Big brand Conscious Marketers.

And this one works…

The soap brand Savlon addressed the issue of sanitation and the spread of deadly germs in India by creating chalk sticks made of soap for children to use in schools. So as the kids do their lessons, they are actually also washing their hands. Savlon is a Conscious Marketer. A local brand Conscious Marketer.

And this one works…

To help combat plastic pollution in oceans and its devastating impact on sea life, craft beer brand Saltwater Brewery in Florida created six-pack rings/holders that are completely biodegradable and edible, made from barley and wheat ribbons from the brewing process. No more plastic holders! Saltwater Brewery is a Conscious Marketer. A small brand Conscious Marketer.

All great examples of brands doing the hard work without asking for anything from their consumers.

Globally and locally...

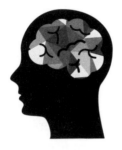

conscious acculturation

YOUR BUTT AND YOUR BRAIN

Don't let your butt dominate your brain.
—Chinese proverb

ACCULTURATION. THAT'S A BIG WORD with a whole lot of meaning. But it's not a buzzword, because I'm not sure that most marketers embrace it into their plans. Not yet, anyway.

I'm sure you won't be surprised to hear that, yet again, acculturation is a big part of being conscious, particularly if you run a global (multimarket) brand.

Let's begin again with our friends at Wikipedia.

Acculturation: "The process of social, psychological, and cultural change that stems from blending between cultures. The effects of acculturation can be seen at multiple levels in both the original and newly adopted cultures."

That's a definition with big words and a whole lot of meaning. Let's break it down.

For me, acculturation is getting to know other cultures that are different from my own and embracing some of the customs, behaviors, and attitudes.

I practice acculturation both personally and professionally.

Whenever I visit a new country, I try to learn and embrace the most interesting parts of its culture. In my work, I have a global role, so part of my job is acculturation of the many office locations in our network. I have to be conscious of my teams' differing cultures and embrace each and every one of them. Equally.

Sometimes acculturation goes beyond just embracing the cultural differences to also adopting them into my own life— like the food, or the music, or the business customs.

Part of being a Conscious Marketer is acculturation. Purposeful acculturation. Tailored acculturation. Conscious acculturation, from a global perspective as well as a local one, and vice versa.

Part of being conscious is also being global, even when you're local. I know that might not make sense when you first read it but being global also means understanding how your locality fits in with what's going on globally. While you might sit in one place, how does your "place" fit into the rest of the world?

Being conscious means understanding the cultural differences around the world and not just thinking that your way of thinking is the only thinking around.

See the thinking?

I heard a famous (or perhaps infamous) Chinese proverb at

we tend to view the world from wherever we sit

a conference I was attending, and it instantly became one of my favorite sayings. One of my colleagues from China used it as the theme of her presentation. She had me at "hello."

It loosely translates to, "Don't let your butt dominate your brain."

It essentially says that we tend to view the world from wherever we sit.

Our butts can sometimes dominate our brains.

We sometimes see the world through local eyes, and those local eyes cloud our global perceptions.

Our butts dominate our brains.

So as a result, we make decisions, marketing decisions, based solely on what's going on locally.

Our butts dominate our brains.

In Conscious Marketing, we can't let our butts dominate our brains.

When we are managing and growing a global brand, we have to account for global differences. What works in one market might not ring true in another. So we have to consciously understand cultures from all around the world, not just our home market. And we have to acculturate the brand experience from market to market, much like we tailor the experience from touchpoint to touchpoint.

We talked about the brand Coca-Cola earlier in the book.

Coca-Cola is a master at acculturation. All around the world, the brand stands for happiness but in a different way in each market. Coca-Cola in Mexico (its second-largest market in the world) translates happiness differently than in the United States (its largest market in the world) and differently in Asia (its fastest-growing market in the world). But even within a market, we see the Coca-Cola brand try to acculturate different cultures within that single culture, showing how the brand brings us all together to be happy. Culturally happy!

Cola-Cola is a Conscious Marketer and doesn't let its butt dominate its brain.

Granted, we still need local marketing and can still offer a local perspective, and we definitely have to do that uniquely in each market. But it still has to ladder up to a global strategy so that the overall branding is consistent from market to market. So while we are doing local marketing, we have to keep a global perspective.

Just like Coca-Cola.

The only way to do that is by being conscious of each and every culture where you plan to market and seeing how that culture varies from what you might consider to be home base. You need "feet on the street," shall we say, who can give you the local acculturation. But those "feet" have to have a global "head."

It all starts with being conscious, once again—globally conscious and locally conscious. Something any and all of us in marketing need to do.

Just like Coca-Cola.

But you don't have to be a big global brand to do it...

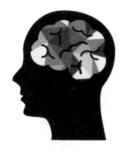

not just for big brands

SMALL BUSINESS CONSCIOUSNESS

The important thing is not being afraid to take a chance. Remember, the greatest failure is to not try. Once you find something you love to do, be the best at doing it.
—Debbie Fields, founder of Mrs. Fields Cookies

I'VE ALWAYS WORKED ON big brands. Even though I consider myself to be an entrepreneur, and I advise other entrepreneurs, I have generally worked on big global brands for my entire career.

So as a result, I tend to write and discuss from a big brand perspective, but the truth is that Conscious Marketing is applicable to brands of all sizes.

It's not the size of the revenue or the size of the marketing budget that matters at all. Anything and everything is a brand.

What matters is that you apply the principles we've discussed in this book to your business, any business. It doesn't always even involve money; much of marketing simply relies on hard work, regardless of the spend.

It's often said that small business is the backbone of the American economy—and the world economy as well. I couldn't agree more. We tend to see more innovation come from small business owners and entrepreneurs than we do big brands and big corporations. Thanks to the millennial mind-set!

So it's just as important for small businesses to be conscious as well.

In fact, I could easily argue that being a Conscious Marketer is actually easier for small businesses. But the consciousness shouldn't be any smaller as a result. In fact, if anything, the consciousness is even bigger.

As an entrepreneur, you're even closer to your consumers.

As an entrepreneur, you can make your marketing so much more personal. You probably share the same values with your consumers. It should be easier to get to know them and to understand their lives. It should, in theory, be easier to discover and understand the issues that worry them. You can be right in the middle of the pain points, making it easier to identify the tension and relieve it for them personally.

I just recently observed this in action in Brooklyn with a small business owner who owns an ice cream shop. In honor of International Women's Day, the ice cream shop ran a promotion for an $0.80 scoop of ice cream. But only for the women. The $0.80 scoop calls attention to the pay gap that women face because, on average, women earn about 80 percent of what men earn. Wow!

Was I insulted as a guy who loves ice cream? No! I was

impressed as a Conscious Marketer. In fact, I thought to myself, "This little ice cream shop in Brooklyn is a Conscious Marketer."

Who knew?

There's another ice cream shop in Manhattan that is so popular that people line up around the corner to get in: The Big Gay Ice Cream Shoppe. I would argue that there's nothing particularly different about this brand's ice cream except for the name and the T-shirts and the unicorn sprinkles that adorn just about everything. Everyone just wants to be associated with something that open and honest and up front. The brand is hitting an emotional chord of some sort. Isn't that what a brand is?

Now, The Big Gay Ice Cream Shoppe has gone mobile with ice cream trucks, and it's also starting to appear in the freezer sections of some local grocery stores. It's extending the emotional chord beyond its one store.

As shown through these ice cream shops in New York, consumers are at the heart of each small business, much more so than any big brand. As a small business owner, you should have your consumers in your heart, all the time, and you should understand what's important to them.

Example: Mrs. Fields Cookies

Debbie Fields, as founder of Mrs. Fields Cookies, did exactly that, eventually growing to become a much bigger brand. She understood the emotional connection that a fresh homemade cookie can create with consumers, and she leveraged the in-store experience to deliver on it. Her business flourished as locals flocked to her store, and then to multiple stores, well in advance of social media.

You can do what Mrs. Fields did.

Debbie Fields stayed close to her consumers, and you should too. You've got plenty of resources at your disposal to do just that:

- Your customers walking through your "door" (physically or virtually)
- Social media monitoring and participation
- Google analytics to see what's important to your consumers
- Google News (and your custom filters) to see what's happening in your consumers' world

Your consumers should be #everything, but just don't forget about your biggest asset...

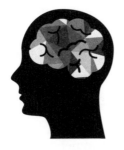

don't forget your employees

INTERNAL CONSCIOUSNESS

Employees who believe that management is concerned about them as a whole person—not just an employee—are more productive, more satisfied, more fulfilled. Satisfied employees mean satisfied customers, which leads to profitability.
—Anne Mulcahy, chairman and CEO of Xerox

BEING A CONSCIOUS MARKETER doesn't just apply to external branding. It's just as important to be conscious of what's going on inside your organization as well as outside of it.

In fact, many argue, and I would be one of the many, that your internal stakeholders are even more important than your external ones. Meaning, when you get employees to embody the brand internally, then you are much more likely to have a successful brand externally with consumers. Your employees become ambassadors and a key component to the overall brand experience. Particularly those employees who touch your consumers.

As a result, your consciousness should start inside.

I just love what the CEO of Xerox once said about thinking of each employee as a "whole person."

Each of our teammates is a complete person, not just someone at work. Not just someone who produces work for the team. Each teammate has an entire life happening, far beyond what we see of him or her at work.

I completely agree, and I'd take it even a step further.

We should treat each of our employees as a unique individual as well. Not only is each teammate a complete person, but he or she is also a unique person. Each is an individual, with an individual existence and an individual experience.

Complete individuals, if you will.

When you think of each of your employees as a whole person, then you are conscious of the fact that his or her work does not solely define who he or she is. Each and every one of us has a whole lot of things going on in the background that take up our time and attention. Home life, personal life, social life, health life…gosh, well, life is all-consuming.

So even when work is loaded with demands and deadlines, employees also have other things on their minds. Each and every person is doing a balancing act of duties, and many think it's off-balance. And it most likely is off-balance. Way off-balance, if you use historical societal norms for work/life balance.

So, as an employer, if you can be conscious of that balancing act when asking for productivity from your team, then you'll have a better understanding of how to help your employees not only do a better balancing act but also a better job at their work. And hopefully be happier at home.

Happiness at home and at work is the goal for each individual. We must all be conscious of that if we want a successful team.

On the other side, when you treat your employees as unique individuals, then you are conscious of the fact that you can't bucket them into categories and treat them as large groups.

Each and every one of us has a unique mix of skills and experiences that makes us special and that allows us to bring something special to the table. So when you're thinking through the programs you offer to your employees and what it'll take to make them happy and productive, then you must think of them as individuals with individual needs.

The key is to build a diverse group of talent that can bring a diverse set of thinking. And not just diversity in the traditional sense of the word, although that is immensely important. By diversity I mean on many levels including race, background, economics, gender, gender identity, sexual orientation, and the list goes on. It'll never be complete until you continually strive for more diversity.

In addition to each employee being a whole person and a unique individual, each of your employees is also a consumer. Just like we think about the consumers who buy our brands.

Your employees also have to buy your internal brand as well, and they have to understand the functional and emotional benefits that you offer to those who work in the organization. You have to position the company as a great place for them to work, to manage their careers, and to continually learn and develop and grow.

Positioning!

You have to communicate to them clearly and frequently, just like you would for your external consumers. Your employees are soaking up everything you say and do and deciding if it's all working for them. Your employees are consumers. They are consuming where they work, especially when the work is consuming for them!

Communication!

Being conscious of your employees as consumers will force you to operate in the same methodical way in which you market your brand. In fact, you are doing just that: marketing your brand to your internal stakeholders. To your employees and teammates.

Marketing!

My point here is that being conscious means thinking not only externally but also internally. And when you think internally, you can't lump all your employees into one bucket. They are individuals, and they have many other things going on in their lives other than work.

Be conscious of that, and you'll make the team much more successful as a result.

Call it personal consciousness.

A little personal consciousness will help you to be even more successful…

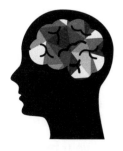

CHAPTER 35

personal consciousness

WHAT'S YOUR EXPERIENCE?

Do one thing every day that scares you.
—Anonymous

SO NOW IT'S UP TO YOU.

Start being even more conscious about your marketing than perhaps you have been to date. Start paying more attention to the issues that your consumers care about. Figure out how your brand can contribute more to the satisfaction of your consumers' lives. Treat your internal consumers as individuals and as whole people.

Real people.

Get real conscious about it all.

If it makes sense, take a stand on an issue. But only if it makes sense.

Above all else, make it personal.

Get to know your consumers personally as human beings, not just as people who are buying your "stuff." Make a connection with them about the things that matter most to them on a personal level. On a human level.

However, while I say to make it personal, don't let your personal convictions cloud your branding judgment.

Being a Conscious Marketer means understanding what's important to your consumers, not what's important to you. It's not about your point of view; it's about their points of view. While your personal views may purposefully align with your brand views and with your consumers' views, it's still about how they see the world, not how you personally see it.

Remember also that as a leader, it's not about you, either. The brand should be about its consumers, not about its leaders. As a brand leader, put your consumers first. Put your teammates first as well.

You know the guy at the cocktail party who only talks about himself? You stay with him for just a few minutes, and then you realize that he's only into himself. So you leave. You're not buying it.

Don't be that guy.

For social interactions, I follow the 90/10 rule.

Ninety percent of the time I talk about the person I'm talking to, and 10 percent of the time I talk about myself. Or at least I try. I might not always be successful, but I try. There are times when it's about me, but I try to keep those to a minimum. I hope my friends and colleagues would agree. Okay, maybe it's more like 80/20 or 75/25, but you get the point!

Put your teammates first

Talk more about them than you talk about yourself, no matter the ratio.

But at the same time, become more personally involved and active in the communities where your consumers thrive, and live right alongside each and every one of them. Both your internal and external consumers. As a brand and as a person... you'll reap rewards all around, and they will too.

Start now. Start today. Start becoming a Conscious Marketer.

Read the news every morning and track the social feeds every day. Follow your consumers as they go about their days and nights, through their work and home lives. Learn from each interaction, and learn how you can become more conscious in your brand's marketing

What's going on in the world that affects them? How do they feel about it?

What are their opinions, triumphs, and frustrations? How do they express them?

What are the emotional benefits that your brand can uniquely offer to them?

What do they want from your brand?

Where are the pain points?

Where's the tension that your brand can solve—uniquely?

How can your brand relieve tension?

Will that relief build loyalty?

How are you going to build an emotional connection that bonds your brand to your consumers for life?

And ultimately: What's your experience? What's your conscious experience?

Finally, approach each interaction with humility.

To me, being a humble person is being a conscious person. People who are humble are much more enjoyable to be around because they aren't "that guy" at the party, and they aren't just all about themselves. Even when they have a success, they attribute it to those around them and those who support them.

Being humble is a gift—for yourself and for all your consumers.

Being humble is what will help you become the best of the best...

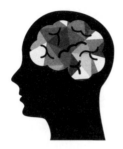

be a benchmark brand

CONSCIOUS LOYALTY

*Your premium brand had better be delivering something
special, or it's not going to get the business.*
—Warren Buffet, CEO of Berkshire Hathaway

ONE FINAL THOUGHT BEFORE WE DEPART.

The final result, from a business perspective, of being a
Conscious Marketer is brand loyalty.

We want our consumers to come back to us—every single
time they need us—because they want to. Both the consumers
who buy our external brand and our employees who buy our

internal brand. Brand loyalty is the ultimate goal, but please remember that consumers need products but they want brands.

Loyalty is royalty when being a Conscious Marketer.

We used to think that brand loyalty meant that our consumers bought our products every single time they needed it out of default, without ever considering another option. Being loyal meant passively going back to the same product time and time again because it was easy. It was routine.

That kind of loyalty worked at the time. We sold stuff, over and over again. Being a default brand meant that our products had consumer loyalty.

In Conscious Marketing, that definition of loyalty doesn't work anymore.

All it takes is for a competitor to come along with a more compelling emotional benefit, and bam, your product is out of consideration. The repetitive passive purchasing stops. Something else came along that was better. Something else had a better positioning that was more relevant.

Conscious loyalty is when consumers choose the brand every single time—purposefully. Consciously. Thoughtfully. Because they've thought about it consciously, and your brand still remains the best option.

They want your brand, consciously.

With this kind of conscious loyalty, your brand becomes the benchmark in the category, and the one to beat! Your brand becomes the standard to which all others are compared. But because it's a conscious decision, as marketers, we have to prove ourselves each time. Each time consumers purchase, they're thinking about your brand and comparing it. It's all very active. It's all very conscious.

It keeps us marketers on our toes, forcing us to be the best we can be. It keeps us conscious of how our consumers are changing and how we need to change to keep relevant.

Now, loyalty is not about being a default brand but being a benchmark brand.

Benchmark brands are the best option out there. Benchmark brands give the best experience for all constituents involved. Benchmark brands are Conscious Marketers.

Consumers are going to choose Conscious Marketers time and time again, making them the benchmark in the category.

Are you a benchmark brand?

What's your experience?

#Done

Marketing is a spectator sport...

...hope you learned something new today!

JimJoseph.com

about
jim joseph

THE CONSCIOUS MARKETER AND
OUT AND ABOUT DAD

JimJoseph.com

Jim is a modern-day renaissance man, running a successful agency, speaking regularly, teaching at NYU, and contributing to Entrepreneur Magazine *and other leading-edge business publications. He's the real deal when it comes to personal branding, PR, and marketing. Above all, he's a nice guy!*
—A LinkedIn endorsement for Jim Joseph

MARKETING IS A SPECTATOR SPORT, and Jim Joseph is one of the industry's most engaging, enthralling, and entertaining commentators. As a global leader in the marketing and communications industry, Jim constantly puts his experience to the test. His consistent goal throughout his career has been to help blockbuster clients, including Kellogg's, Kraft, Ford, Johnson & Johnson, Sonic, IKEA, AFLAC, Walmart, and Microsoft, create successful brand experiences that engage consumers and add value to their lives.

Jim is the award-winning author of *The Experience Effect* series as well as the award-winning personal memoir *Out and About Dad*, where he chronicles his journey as a father during a unique time in our cultural evolution. He is also an adjunct instructor at New York University, where he teaches a graduate class in integrated marketing.

"When you've got something that needs to get done, give it to someone who's busy!"

Entrepreneur of the Year, Agency of the Year, Consumer Launch Campaign of the Year, Most Creative Agency, Best Place to Work, Social Media Icon, Hall of Fame—these are the accolades that Jim Joseph has amassed through his long career in marketing. But none are more important than the daily badge he wears with the most pride: Dad.